THE PRECIOUS TREASURY OF THE BASIC SPACE OF PHENOMENA

THE SEVEN TREASURIES SERIES

This series consists of the volumes written by Longchen Rabjam that, as a group, have come to be known as *The Seven Treasuries*. Although Longchenpa did not intend them to be a series, scholars traditionally treat them as such because of their interrelated themes.

Published Volumes

The Precious Treasury of the Way of Abiding

A Treasure Trove of Scriptural Transmission

The Precious Treasury of the Basic Space of Phenomena

Longchen Rabjam

Translated under the direction of
His Eminence Chagdud Tulku Rinpoche
by Richard Barron (Lama Chökyi Nyima)

Edited by members of
the Padma Translation Committee:
Susanne Fairclough, Jeff Miller,
Mary Racine, and Robert Racine

PADMA PUBLISHING

2001

Published by Padma Publishing
P.O. Box 279
Junction City, California 96048-0279

Printed in the United States of America

Second Printing 2003

Jacket design by Daniel Tesser

Library of Congress Cataloging in Publication Data

Kloṅ-chen-pa Dri-med-'od-zer, 1308–1363
The precious treasury of the basic space of phenomena / by Longchen Rabjam; translated under the direction of His Eminence Chagdud Tulku Rinpoche by Richard Barron (Chökyi Nyima); edited by members of the Padma Translation Committee: Susanne Fairclough . . . [et al.]

p. cm.

ISBN 1-881847-32-2

1. Tantric Buddhism—Tibet. I. Barron, Richard II. Title.
BQ8918.2.K57 2001
294.3′420423—dc21 2001021330

Foreword

His Eminence Chagdud Tulku Rinpoche

The publication of Longchen Rabjam's *Seven Treasuries* should be a cause for rejoicing among deeply committed English-speaking Buddhists who aspire to realize the *dzogchen,* or great perfection, teachings of vajrayana Buddhism. Though there are many spiritual traditions in this world, Buddhism offers the deepest examination of what constitutes the root of samsara, and of how to deal with all levels of obscuration and attain liberation. Among Buddhist teachings, none are more profound, more capable of freeing the mind from its most subtle obscurations, than those of the great perfection.

Yet, because great perfection transmission leads to wisdom beyond words and concepts, the translation of dzogchen texts presents tremendous difficulties. Some lamas have said that it is not even worth the attempt, that too much distortion results. I respect their opinion, but feel that those of us with the supreme fortune to have received authentic transmission from great dzogchen masters have a responsibility to maintain the oral lineage, including the translation of texts, as well as the mind-to-mind lineage of realization. If we eschew this work, the precious great perfection teachings will remain inaccessible to some excellent Western practitioners who have potential as meditators but who do not know Tibetan. An avenue for the flourishing of the transmission will be cut off.

I am also gravely concerned about the translations of great perfection texts produced by Westerners who know Tibetan but who rely solely on scholarly knowledge, without recourse to teachers. Intellectual understanding alone, without the ripening process that takes place under the direction of qualified dzogchen teachers, will certainly result in misguided translations, perpetuated in misguided meditation by those who base their spiritual practice on such translations. But again, if qualified dzogchen masters refrain from working on translations because they fear imperfect results, can they lament when even more erroneous translations are published?

The translator of these texts, Richard Barron (Lama Chökyi Nyima), has truly mastered both literary and spoken Tibetan, but his deeper understanding is based on an extended retreat under the guidance of His Eminence Kalu Rinpoche, on a number of six-week dzogchen retreats, and on listening to and translating the teachings of many eminent lamas. He has translated other great perfection texts and sadhanas, notably Dudjom Lingpa's *Buddhahood Without Meditation,* under my direction. He thus brings more capability to his work than mere theoretical and intellectual competence. The other members of the translation committee have a grounding in the study of dzogchen terminology and have likewise participated in annual dzogchen retreats. The learned scholar Khenpo Chödzö has been consulted on many details of this translation of *The Precious Treasury of the Basic Space of Phenomena.* I myself have brought to the process whatever understanding of great perfection I have attained in the course of a lifetime of study and meditation.

This means that while we have not necessarily produced flawless translations, we have confidence in this groundbreaking attempt. It should be understood that works of this kind are not casually read and easily comprehended. In fact, for most people, the texts are quite difficult to fathom; their meaning unfolds according to the depth of the reader's spiritual preparation. However, simply having these books in one's home is more valuable than having statues or stupas, for they are truly relics of the dharmakaya. Such holy works carry powerful blessings and are worthy objects of faith and devotion.

The project of translating Longchen Rabjam's *Seven Treasuries* is ongoing. We encourage anyone with knowledge and experience of the great perfection to contact us with suggestions, clarifications, or corrections, which we will consider for incorporation into future editions. May these precious texts illuminate the minds of all who read and venerate them.

Translation Committee's Note

Among the works in Longchen Rabjam's famous collection, *The Seven Treasuries,* is that commonly known as the *Chöying Dzöd*, which consists of two texts: a set of source verses entitled *The Precious Treasury of the Basic Space of Phenomena* and Longchenpa's own commentary on those verses, *A Treasure Trove of Scriptural Transmission.* Although we have published them individually, they are considered companion volumes.

Details concerning the Tibetan verses in the present volume can be found in the endnotes to the commentary.

Longchen Rabjam

The Precious Treasury of the Basic Space of Phenomena

༄༅། །ཆོས་དབྱིངས་རིན་པོ་ཆེའི་མཛོད་ཅེས་བྱ་བ་བཞུགས།

In Sanskrit: *Dharmadhātu ratna koṣa nāma*

།རྒྱ་གར་སྐད་དུ། དྷརྨ་དྷཱ་ཏུ་རཏྣ་ཀོ་ཥ་ནཱ་མ།

In Tibetan: *Chos dbyings rin po che'i mdzod ces bya ba*

བོད་སྐད་དུ། ཆོས་དབྱིངས་རིན་པོ་ཆེའི་མཛོད་ཅེས་བྱ་བ།

དཔལ་ཀུན་ཏུ་བཟང་པོ་ལ་ཕྱག་འཚལ་ལོ།

།གདོད་ནས་ལྷུན་གྲུབ་ངོ་མཚར་རྨད་ཀྱི་ཆོས། །རང་བྱུང་ཡེ་ཤེས་འོད་གསལ་བྱང་ཆུབ་སེམས། །སྣང་སྲིད་སྣོད་བཅུད་འཁོར་འདས་འབྱུང་བའི་མཛོད། །མི་གཡོ་སྤྲོས་དང་བྲལ་ལ་ཕྱག་འཚལ་ལོ།

།ཐེག་པའི་ཡང་རྩེ་རི་རྒྱལ་ཉི་ཟླའི་གླིང་། །འོད་གསལ་ལྷུན་གྲུབ་རྡོ་རྗེ་སྙིང་པོའི་གླིང་། །རྩོལ་ཞིང་སྒྲུབ་མེད་རང་བཞིན་བབས་ཀྱི་གླིང་། །ཡེ་འབྱམས་རྨད་དུ་བྱུང་བ་བཤད་ཀྱིས་ཉོན།།

།།ལྷུན་གྲུབ་གླིང་ལས་ཐམས་ཅད་འབྱུང་བའི་གཞི། །ངོ་བོ་སྟོང་ལ་རང་བཞིན་མ་འགགས་པ། །ཅིར་ཡང་མ་གྲུབ་ཅིར་ཡང་འཆར་བ་སྟེ། །

HOMAGE TO GLORIOUS SAMANTABHADRA!

Naturally occurring timeless awareness—utterly lucid
awakened mind—
is something marvelous and superb, primordially and
spontaneously present.
It is the treasury from which comes the universe of appearances
and possibilities, whether of samsara or nirvana.
Homage to that unwavering state, free of elaboration.

The very pinnacle of spiritual approaches, the expanse in which
the sun and moon orbit the most majestic mountain,
is the expanse of the vajra heart essence—spontaneously present
and utterly lucid—
the expanse of the naturally settled state that entails no effort or
achievement.
Listen as I explain this superb, timelessly infinite expanse.

❖

WITHIN THE EXPANSE of spontaneous presence is the ground
for all that arises.
Empty in essence, continuous by nature,
it has never existed as anything whatsoever, yet arises as
anything at all.

སྐུ་གསུམ་ཀློང་ནས་འཁོར་འདས་རང་ཤར་ཀྱང་། །དབྱིངས་ལས་མ་གཡོས་ཆོས་ཉིད་བདེ་བའི་ཞིང་།

།སེམས་ཉིད་ཀློང་ཆེན་འགྱུར་མེད་ནམ་མཁའི་དང་། །རོལ་པ་ངེས་མེད་ཐུགས་རྗེ་ཆོ་འཕྲུལ་ཀློང་། །ཐམས་ཅད་དབྱིངས་ཀྱི་རྒྱན་ལས་ལོག་ན་མེད། །ཕྱི་ནང་འདུ་འཕྲོ་བྱང་ཆུབ་སེམས་ཀྱི་རྩལ། །ཅིར་ཡང་མ་ཡིན་ཅིར་ཡང་འཆར་བའི་ཕྱིར། །ངོ་མཚར་ཆོ་འཕྲུལ་ཡ་མཚན་རྨད་ཀྱི་ཆོས།

།ཕྱི་ནང་སྐྱེ་འགྲོ་གཟུགས་སུ་སྣང་བ་ཀུན། །དབྱིངས་ཀྱི་རྒྱན་དེ་སྐུ་ཡི་འཁོར་ལོར་ཤར། །མ་ལུས་གྲགས་པའི་སྒྲ་སྐད་ཇི་སྙེད་ཀུན། །དབྱིངས་ཀྱི་རྒྱན་དེ་གསུང་གི་འཁོར་ལོར་ཤར། །དྲན་རིག་འགྱུ་འཕྲོ་མི་རྟོག་བསམ་ཡས་ཀྱང་། །དབྱིངས་ཀྱི་རྒྱན་དེ་ཐུགས་ཀྱི་འཁོར་ལོར་ཤར།

།འགྲོ་བ་རིགས་དྲུག་སྐྱེ་གནས་བཞི་པོ་ཡང་། །ཆོས་དབྱིངས་དང་ལས་གཡོས་པ་རྡུལ་ཙམ་མེད། །སྣང་སྲིད་ཡུལ་དྲུག་གཟུང་འཛིན་སྣང་བ་ཡང་། །ཆོས་དབྱིངས་དང་ན་མེད་སྣང་སྒྱུ་མའི་ཚུལ། །

Within the expanse of the three kayas, although samsara and
nirvana arise naturally,
they do not stray from basic space—such is the blissful realm
that is the true nature of phenomena.

Mind itself is a vast expanse, the realm of unchanging space.
Its indeterminate display is the expanse of the magical
expression of its responsiveness.
Everything is the adornment of basic space and nothing else.
Outwardly and inwardly, things proliferating and resolving are
the dynamic energy of awakened mind.
Because this is nothing whatsoever yet arises as anything at all,
it is a marvelous and magical expression, amazing and superb.

Throughout the entire universe, all beings and all that manifests
as form
are adornments of basic space, arising as the ongoing principle
of enlightened form.
What is audible, all sounds and voices without exception,
as many as there may be,
are adornments of basic space, arising as the ongoing principle
of enlightened speech.
All consciousness and all stirring and proliferation of thoughts,
as well as the inconceivable range of nonconceptual states,
are adornments of basic space, arising as the ongoing principle
of enlightened mind.

Beings born in the six classes through the four avenues of rebirth,
moreover,
do not stray in the slightest from the basic space of phenomena.
The universe of appearances and possibilities—
the six kinds of sense objects manifesting in dualistic
perception—
appears within the realm of the basic space of phenomena just as
illusions do, manifest yet nonexistent.

རྟེན་མེད་སང་སེང་ཡེ་སྟོང་ཡངས་པ་ཆེ། །རང་གསལ་ཇི་བཞིན་ཆོས་དབྱིངས་རྒྱན་དུ་ཤར།

།ཇི་ལྟར་སྣང་གྲགས་དབྱིངས་ཀྱི་ངང་ཆེན་འདིར། །ལྷུན་མཉམ་མི་གཡོ་ཆོས་སྐུ་བྱང་ཆུབ་སེམས། །ཡེ་བབས་རང་སྟོང་འཕོ་དང་འགྱུར་མེད་པས། །ཅིར་སྣང་ཆོས་ཉིད་རང་བྱུང་ཡེ་ཤེས་དང་། །བྱ་དང་རྩོལ་མེད་བདེ་ཀློང་གཅིག་ཏུ་འཁྲིལ།

།རང་གསལ་མི་གཡོ་ལོངས་སྤྱོད་རྫོགས་པ་ནི། །གང་སྣང་ཉིད་ནས་རང་བཞིན་ལྷུན་གྱིས་གྲུབ། །བཅོས་ཤིང་བསྒྱུར་མེད་ལྷུན་མཉམ་གདལ་བའོ།

།སྣ་ཚོགས་མ་འདྲེས་རོལ་པའི་འཆར་ཚུལ་ལས། །སྤྲུལ་པ་རང་བྱུང་ཡ་མཚན་འཕྲུལ་གྱི་དོན། །བྱ་བྲལ་ཀུན་ཏུ་བཟང་ལས་གཡོས་པ་མེད།

།གཡང་ས་མེད་པའི་བྱང་ཆུབ་སེམས་ཉིད་ལ། །རྩོལ་བ་མེད་པའི་སྐུ་གསུམ་ལྷུན་རྫོགས་ཀྱང་། །དབྱིངས་ལས་མ་གཡོས་ལྷུན་གྲུབ་འདུས་མ་བྱས། །སྐུ་དང་ཡེ་ཤེས་ཁྲིན་ལས་ལྷུན་རྫོགས་ཀྱང་། །ཚོགས་ཆེན་ཡེ་རྫོགས་ཡེ་ཤར་ཆེན་པོའི་ཀློང་།

Without underlying support, vividly apparent yet timelessly
empty, supremely spacious, and naturally clear, just as it is,
the universe arises as the adornment of the basic space of
phenomena.

However things appear or sound, within the vast realm of
basic space
they do not stray from their spontaneous equalness as
dharmakaya, awakened mind.
Since the timeless state of utter relaxation is naturally empty
and without transition or change,
whatever manifests constitutes the scope of naturally occurring
timeless awareness, the true nature of phenomena,
merging in a single blissful expanse, without any effort, without
anything needing to be done.

Sambhogakaya is unwavering natural lucidity.
Even as anything at all manifests, it is by nature spontaneously
present,
uncontrived and unadulterated—a pervasive state of
spontaneous equalness.

Due to the way in which the distinct, myriad display arises,
emanations occur naturally—the amazing magic of what has
ultimate meaning.
They never stray from the wholly positive state in which nothing
need be done.

Within awakened mind itself, which is without pitfalls,
the spontaneous perfection of the three kayas, entailing
no effort,
is such that, without straying from basic space, they are
spontaneously present and uncompounded.
The spontaneous perfection of the kayas, timeless awareness,
and enlightened activity, moreover,
is a great amassing—the supreme expanse that is timelessly
perfect, timelessly arising.

།ཡེ་ནས་ལྷུན་གྲུབ་འཕོ་འགྱུར་མེད་པའི་ཞིང་། །ཆོས་དབྱིངས་དང་ལས་ཆོས་ཉིད་གཟིགས་པ་ཡང་། །མཁྱེན་པ་མ་འགགས་དབྱིངས་ཀྱི་རྒྱན་དུ་ཤར། །བྱས་ཤིང་སྒྲུབ་མེད་ཡེ་ནས་གནས་པ་ཉིད། །ཉི་མཁའ་བཞིན་དེ་ངོ་མཚར་རྨད་ཀྱི་ཆོས།

།ཡེ་ནས་ལྷུན་གྱིས་གྲུབ་པའི་དབྱིངས་རུམ་འདིར། །འཁོར་བ་ཀུན་བཟང་མྱ་ངན་འདས་པ་བཟང་། །ཀུན་བཟང་ཀློང་ན་འཁོར་འདས་ཡེ་ནས་མེད། །སྣང་བ་ཀུན་བཟང་སྟོང་པ་ཀུན་ཏུ་བཟང་། །ཀུན་བཟང་ཀློང་ན་སྣང་སྟོང་ཡེ་ནས་མེད། །སྐྱེ་ཤི་ཀུན་བཟང་བདེ་སྡུག་ཀུན་ཏུ་བཟང་། །ཀུན་བཟང་ཀློང་ན་སྐྱེ་ཤི་བདེ་སྡུག་མེད། །བདག་གཞན་ཀུན་བཟང་རྟག་ཆད་ཀུན་ཏུ་བཟང་། །ཀུན་བཟང་ཀློང་ན་བདག་གཞན་རྟག་ཆད་མེད།

།མེད་ལ་ཡོད་པར་འཛིན་པས་འཁྲུལ་པར་བཏགས། །ཧེན་མེད་རྨི་ལམ་འདྲ་བའི་རང་བཞིན་ལ། །འཁོར་འདས་རང་མཚན་ཞེན་པ་མཚར་རེ་ཆེ།

།ཐམས་ཅད་ཀུན་བཟང་ལྷུན་གྲུབ་ཆེན་པོ་ཡིན། །མ་འཁྲུལ་མི་འཁྲུལ་འཁྲུལ་པར་མི་འགྱུར་བས། །སྲིད་པ་མིང་ཙམ་ཡོད་མེད་མཐའ་ལས་འདས།

།

Timelessly and spontaneously present, this pure realm is
without transition or change.
With the perception of the true nature of phenomena within
basic space,
wisdom arises continuously as the adornment of that space.
Not created or achieved, it abides timelessly.
Like the sun in the sky, it is amazing and superb.

Within this ultimate womb of basic space, timelessly and
spontaneously present,
samsara is wholly positive, nirvana is positive.
Within the wholly positive expanse, samsara and nirvana have
never existed.
Sensory appearances are wholly positive, emptiness is positive.
Within the wholly positive expanse, appearances and emptiness
have never existed.
Birth and death are wholly positive, happiness and suffering
are positive.
Within the wholly positive expanse, birth, death, happiness,
and suffering have never existed.
Self and other are wholly positive, affirmation and negation
are positive.
Within the wholly positive expanse, self, other, affirmation,
and negation have never existed.

Labeling takes place in confusion, for what is nonexistent is
taken to exist.
Given that the nature of things is similar to that of dream images,
which have no basis,
how exceedingly strange it is to fixate on samsara and nirvana
as though they existed in their own right!

Everything is wholly positive, a supreme state of spontaneous
presence.
Since there never has been confusion, is no confusion, and never
will be confusion,
conditioned existence is merely a label.

སུ་ཡང་གང་དུ་སྟོར་ཡང་མ་འཁྲུལ་ལ། །ད་ལྟ་མི་འཁྲུལ་སྐད་ཀྱིས་འཁྲུལ་མི་འགྱུར། །འདི་ནི་སྲིད་གསུམ་ཀ་དག་དགོངས་པའོ།

།འཁྲུལ་པ་མེད་པས་མ་འཁྲུལ་ཆོས་སུ་མེད། །ཡེ་ནས་ལྷུན་གྲུབ་རང་བྱུང་རིག་པ་ཆེ། །མ་གྲོལ་མི་གྲོལ་གྲོལ་བར་མི་འགྱུར་བས། །འདས་པ་མིང་ཙམ་སུ་ཡང་གྲོལ་མ་མྱོང་། །གྲོལ་བར་མི་འགྱུར་བཅིངས་པ་ཡེ་ནས་མེད། །མཁའ་བཞིན་རྣམ་དག་རྒྱ་ཆད་ཕྱོགས་ལྷུང་བྲལ། །འདི་ནི་ཡོངས་གྲོལ་ཀ་དག་དགོངས་པའོ།

།མདོར་ན་ལྷུན་གྲུབ་ཡངས་པའི་དབྱིངས་རུམ་ནས། །རོལ་པའི་རྩལ་གྱི་འཁོར་འདས་ཅི་ཤར་ཡང་། །ཤར་ཙམ་ཉིད་ནས་འཁོར་འདས་ཡོད་མ་མྱོང་། །གཉིད་ཀྱི་རྩལ་ལས་རྨི་ལམ་ཅི་ཤར་ཡང་། །དོན་ལ་མེད་དེ་རང་རིག་བདེ་བའི་མལ། །ལྷུན་མཉམ་ཡངས་པ་ཆེན་པོར་ཕྱམ་གདལ་ལོ།

།ཆོས་དབྱིངས་རིན་པོ་ཆེའི་མཛོད་ལས། །འཁོར་འདས་དབྱིངས་ལས་མ་གཡོས་པར་བསྟན་པའི་ལེའུ་སྟེ་དང་པོའོ།།

It is beyond the extremes of existence and nonexistence.
Since no one has ever been confused at all in the past,
no one is confused at present and no one will be confused later on.
This is the enlightened intent of the original purity of the three planes of conditioned existence.

Since there is no confusion, nothing exists as some unconfused state.
Supreme, naturally occurring awareness is timelessly and spontaneously present.
Since there never has been freedom, is no freedom, and never will be freedom,
nirvana is just a label and there is no one who has ever known freedom.
There never will be freedom, for there never has been bondage.
Complete purity, like space, is free of being restricted or localized.
This is the enlightened intent of the original purity of total freedom.

In brief, within the ultimate womb of basic space, spacious and spontaneously present,
whatever arises as the dynamic energy of its display—as samsara or nirvana—
in the very moment of simply arising has never known existence as samsara or nirvana.
Whatever arises in a dream due to the dynamic energy of sleep does not actually exist.
There is only self-knowing awareness, the blissful place of rest,
extending infinitely as the supremely spacious state of spontaneous equalness.

This is the first section of *The Precious Treasury of the Basic Space of Phenomena*, demonstrating that samsara and nirvana by nature do not stray from basic space.

༎དབྱིངས་ཀྱི་རང་བཞིན་གདོད་ནས་ལྷུན་གྲུབ་ལ། །ཕྱི་དང་ནང་མེད་ཀུན་ཏུ་ཁྱབ་པར་གདལ། །མཐའ་ཡི་སྨུ་མེད་སྟེང་འོག་ཕྱོགས་མཚམས་འདས། །ཡངས་དོག་གཉིས་མེད་རིག་པ་མཁའ་ལྟར་དག །དམིགས་བསམ་སྤྲོ་བསྡུ་བྲལ་བའི་ཀློང་ཉིད་དོ།

།སྐྱེ་མེད་དབྱིངས་ལས་སྐྱེ་བའི་ཆོ་འཕྲུལ་རྣམས། །ཅིར་ཡང་མ་ངེས་གར་ཡང་རྒྱ་ཆད་མེད། །འདི་ཞེས་མི་མཚོན་དངོས་པོ་མཚན་མ་མེད། །ཕྱོགས་འབྱམས་ནམ་མཁའ་འདྲ་བའི་རང་བཞིན་ལ། །སྐྱེ་མེད་ལྷུན་གྲུབ་སྔ་ཕྱི་ཐོག་མཐའ་བྲལ།

།འཁོར་འདས་ཀུན་གྱི་ངོ་བོ་བྱང་ཆུབ་སེམས། །མ་བྱུང་མ་སྐྱེས་མ་ངེས་ལྷུན་གྲུབ་ནི། །གང་ནས་མ་འོངས་གར་ཡང་སོང་བ་མེད། །སྔ་ཕྱི་རིས་མེད་བྱང་ཆུབ་སེམས་ཀྱི་ཀློང་། །འགྲོ་དང་འོང་མེད་ཀུན་ཏུ་ཁྱབ་པར་གདལ།

།ཐོག་མཐའ་དབུས་མེད་ཆོས་ཉིད་དེ་བཞིན་ཉིད། །ཕྱམ་གདལ་མཁའ་མཉམ་དག་པའི་རང་བཞིན་ལ། །ཐོག་མཐའ་མེད་དེ་སྔ་ཕྱིའི་ཡུལ་ལས་འདས། །སྐྱེ་འགག་མེད་དེ་དངོས་པོ་མཚན་མ་མེད། །འགྲོ་འོང་མེད་དེ་འདི་ཞེས་མཚོན་དང་བྲལ། །

Given that basic space is by nature primordially and
spontaneously present,
it is infinitely pervasive, with no division into outer and inner.
Without any limiting boundaries, it is beyond division into
above and below or any other direction.
Beyond the duality of spacious versus narrow, awareness—
pure like space—
is this very expanse, free of the elaborations of a conceptual
framework.

The magical expressions that originate within unborn
basic space
are completely indeterminate and not subject to any
restrictions whatsoever.
They cannot be characterized as "things," for they have
no substance or characteristics.
In that their nature is like the panoramic vista of space,
they are unborn, spontaneously present, and free of any time
frame, any beginning or end.

The essence of all samsara and nirvana is awakened mind.
Spontaneously present—not occurring, not originating, and
not finite—
it has not come from anywhere, nor does it go anywhere at all.
The expanse of awakened mind, with no linear time frame,
does not come or go, for it is infinitely pervasive.

The true nature of phenomena—suchness—has no beginning,
middle, or end.
This state of infinite evenness, equal to space and pure by nature,
has no beginning or end.
It is beyond any time frame.
It is unborn, unceasing, and has no substance or characteristics.
It neither comes nor goes and cannot be characterized as
some "thing."

རྩོལ་ཞིང་སྒྲུབ་མེད་བྱ་བའི་ཆོས་ཀྱིས་སྟོང་། །ཕྱོགས་ཆ་དབུས་མེད་དེ་བཞིན་ཉིད་ཀྱི་གཞི། །དམིགས་མེད་རྒྱུན་ཆད་མེད་པས་མཉམ་པའི་ཀློང་།

།ཐམས་ཅད་ཆོས་ཉིད་མཉམ་པའི་རང་བཞིན་པས། །མཉམ་པའི་ཀློང་ན་མི་གནས་གཅིག་ཀྱང་མེད། །གཅིག་མཉམ་ཀུན་མཉམ་བྱང་ཆུབ་སེམས་ཀྱི་ངང་། །མ་སྐྱེས་མཁའ་མཉམ་ཡངས་པར་ཕྱམ་གདལ་བས། །མཉམ་ཉིད་ངང་ལ་རྒྱུན་ཆད་མེད་པའི་ཕྱིར།

།ལྷུན་གྲུབ་ཕྱོགས་མེད་ཀུན་ཁྱབ་གདལ་བའི་རྫོང་། །སྟེང་འོག་བར་མེད་ཡེ་ཀློང་ཡངས་པའི་རྫོང་། །ཕྱོགས་མེད་ཀུན་ཤོང་སྐྱེ་མེད་ཆོས་སྐུའི་རྫོང་། །མི་འགྱུར་ལྷུན་གྲུབ་རིན་ཆེན་གསང་བའི་རྫོང་། །སྣང་སྲིད་འཁོར་འདས་ཡེ་རྫོང་ཕྱམ་གཅིག་རྫོགས།

།ཕྱོགས་མེད་ཀུན་ཁྱབ་གདལ་བའི་ས་གཞི་ལ། །འཁོར་འདས་རིས་མེད་བྱང་ཆུབ་སེམས་ཀྱི་མཁར། །ཆོས་ཉིད་ཀློང་ཡངས་རྩེ་མོ་ལྷུན་མཐོ་ཞིང་།། མ་བྱས་རང་བཞིན་ཕྱོགས་བཞི་ཡངས་པའི་དཀྱིལ། །རིམ་རྩོལ་བྲལ་བའི་འཇུག་སྒོ་ཤིན་ཏུ་ཡངས།

It involves no effort or achievement or anything needing
to be done.
The ground of suchness itself has no periphery or center.
Since it is nonreferential and uninterrupted, it is the expanse
of equalness.

Since the true nature of all phenomena is equalness,
there is not a single thing that does not abide within the expanse
of that equalness.
The scope of awakened mind is a single state of evenness in
which everything is equal.
Since it is unborn—an infinite evenness so vast that it is equal
to space—
the scope of equalness is without interruption.

Therefore, the fortress of infinite pervasiveness is spontaneously
present and beyond extremes.
The fortress of the spacious and timeless expanse has no division
into higher and lower or in between.
The fortress of unborn dharmakaya encompasses everything
impartially.
The fortress of the precious secret is unchanging and
spontaneously present.
The universe of appearances and possibilities, whether of
samsara or nirvana,
is perfect as the timeless fortress of a single state of equalness.

On this infinite foundation, extending everywhere impartially,
the stronghold of awakened mind does not distinguish between
samsara and nirvana.
Its imposing and lofty summit is the spacious expanse that is
the true nature of phenomena.
At the very center of the panorama of this uncreated nature,
the entranceway that frees one from developmental effort is
wide open.

།ལྷུན་གྲུབ་འབྱོར་བའི་བཀོད་པས་བརྒྱན་པ་དེར། །རང་བྱུང་ཡེ་ཤེས་རྒྱལ་པོ་གདན་ལ་བཞུགས། །འདུ་འཕྲོར་སྣང་བ་ཡེ་ཤེས་རྩལ་རྣམས་ཀུན། །ལྷོན་པོར་གྱུར་པས་ཡུལ་ལ་དབང་བསྒྱུར་ཞིང་། །རང་གནས་བསམ་གཏན་བཙུན་མོ་དམ་པ་དང་། །དགོངས་པ་རང་ཤར་སྲས་དང་བྲན་གཡོག་བཅས། །བདེ་ཆེན་གློང་འཁྲིལ་རང་གསལ་རྟོག་པ་མེད།

།མི་གཡོ་བསམ་བརྗོད་བྲལ་བའི་ངང་ཉིད་ལས། །སྣང་སྲིད་སྣོད་བཅུད་ཀུན་ལ་མངའ་དབང་བསྒྱུར། །ཆོས་དབྱིངས་ཡངས་པའི་ཡུལ་ཁམས་རྒྱ་ཆེའོ།

།ཡུལ་དེར་གནས་ན་ཐམས་ཅད་ཆོས་ཀྱི་སྐུ། །རང་བྱུང་ཡེ་ཤེས་གཅིག་ལས་མ་གཡོས་པར། །མ་བྱས་ཡེ་ཟིན་རྩོལ་སྒྲུབ་འདས་པ་ཉིད། །གྲྭ་ཟུར་མེད་པའི་ཐིག་ལེ་ཟླུམ་པས་ན། །ཇི་བཞིན་དབྱེ་བསལ་མེད་པའི་ཀློང་དུ་འཁྲིལ།

།འགྲོ་དྲུག་གནས་དང་སངས་རྒྱས་ཞིང་ཁམས་ཀྱང་། །གཞན་ན་མེད་དེ་ཆོས་ཉིད་ནམ་མཁའི་ངང་། །རང་གསལ་བྱང་ཆུབ་སེམས་སུ་རོ་གཅིག་པས། །རིག་པའི་ངང་དུ་འཁོར་འདས་ཙུབ་ཆུབ་བོ།

Within that palace, adorned by the spontaneously present
array of wealth,
the king, naturally occurring timeless awareness, sits on his
throne.
All aspects of the dynamic energy of that awareness, manifesting
as thoughts that proliferate and subside,
serve as ministers, exercising control over the domain.
The holy queen, naturally abiding meditative stability,
is accompanied by the royal heirs and servants, naturally arising
enlightened intent.
This encompassing expanse of supreme bliss is naturally lucid
and nonconceptual.

Within that very context, unwavering and beyond imagination
or description,
mastery is gained over the entire universe of appearances
and possibilities.
This is the vast dominion of the basic space of phenomena.

If one abides in that domain, everything is dharmakaya.
With no wavering from this single, naturally occurring timeless
awareness,
there is an unfabricated, timelessly ensured transcendence of
effort and achievement.
Given that the sphere of being, without any "hard edges,"
is inclusive,
everything, just as it is, is encompassed within the expanse in
which there is no differentiation or exclusion.

Neither the realms of the six classes of beings nor even the pure
realms of buddhas exist elsewhere.
They are the realm of space, the true nature of phenomena.
Given that they are of one taste in naturally lucid awakened
mind,
samsara and nirvana are fully encompassed within the scope
of awareness.

།ཐམས་ཅད་ཀུན་འབྱུང་ཆོས་དབྱིངས་མཛོད་འདི་ན། །འདས་པ་མ་བཙལ་ཡེ་ནས་ལྷུན་གྲུབ་པས། །ཆོས་སྐུ་མི་འགྱུར་ཡུལ་མེད་ཀུན་འབྱམས་ལ།། ཕྱི་ནང་སྣོད་བཅུད་སྣང་བ་ལོངས་སྤྱོད་རྫོགས། །གཟུགས་བརྙན་ལྷ་བུར་རང་ཤར་སྤྲུལ་པའི་སྐུ། །སྐུ་གསུམ་རྒྱན་དུ་མ་རྫོགས་ཆོས་མེད་པས། ། ཐམས་ཅད་སྐུ་གསུང་ཐུགས་ཀྱི་རོལ་པར་ཤར། །བདེ་གཤེགས་ཞིང་ཁམས་མ་ལུས་གྲངས་མེད་ཀྱང་། །ཉིད་ལས་བྱུང་བའི་སེམས་ཉིད་སྐུ་གསུམ་ཀློང་།

།འཁོར་བའི་རང་བཞིན་འགྲོ་དྲུག་གྲོང་ཁྱེར་ཀྱང་། །ཆོས་དབྱིངས་ངང་ལས་གཟུགས་བརྙན་ཤར་བ་ཙམ། །སྐྱེ་ཤི་བདེ་སྡུག་སྣ་ཚོགས་སྣང་བ་ཡང་། །སེམས་ཉིད་ཀློང་འདིར་སྤྲུལ་པའི་ལྟད་མོ་བཞིན། །མེད་ལ་ཡོད་ལ་སྣང་ལ་གཞི་མེད་པས། །མཁའ་ལ་སྤྲིན་བཞིན་གློ་བུར་རྐྱེན་བྱུང་ཙམ། །ཡོད་མིན་མེད་མིན་རང་བཞིན་མཐའ་འདས་པས། །སྤྲོས་བྲལ་ཐིག་ལེའི་ངང་དུ་ཨུབ་ཆུབ་བོ།

།སེམས་ཉིད་བྱང་ཆུབ་སེམས་ཀྱི་རང་བཞིན་ནི། །མཁའ་ལྟར་དག་པས་སྐྱེ་ཤི་བདེ་སྡུག་མེད། །

In this treasury of the basic space of phenomena, the source of everything,
nirvana is timelessly and spontaneously present, without having to be sought.
So within dharmakaya—unchanging, nonreferential, and infinitely extensive—
the manifestation of the outer and inner universe is sambhogakaya,
and the natural arising of things like reflections is nirmanakaya.
Since there is no phenomenon that is not perfect as an adornment of the three kayas,
everything arises as the display of enlightened form, speech, and mind.
Moreover, without exception, the countless pure realms of the sugatas
arise from the very same source—mind itself, the expanse of the three kayas.

As well, the "cities" of the six classes of beings, whose nature is that of samsara,
are simply reflections arising within the scope of the basic space of phenomena.
Moreover, the various manifestations of birth and death, pleasure and pain,
are like phantasmagoria within this expanse—mind itself.
Although they do not exist, they appear to, and in manifesting they have no basis,
and so they are like clouds in the sky, simply occurring adventitiously due to circumstances.
Neither existent nor nonexistent, they are by nature beyond extremes,
fully encompassed within the sphere of being, free of elaboration.

Mind itself—that is, the nature of awakened mind—
is pure like space, and so is without birth or death, pleasure or pain.

དངོས་པོ་རིས་མེད་འཁོར་འདས་ཆོས་ལས་གྲོལ། །འདི་ཞེས་མི་མཚོན་མཁའ་ཀློང་རབ་ཡངས་པས། །མི་འགྱུར་མི་འཕོ་ལྷུན་གྲུབ་འདུས་མ་བྱས། །འོད་གསལ་རྡོ་རྗེ་སྙིང་པོར་སངས་རྒྱས་པས། །ཐམས་ཅད་ཀུན་ཀྱང་རང་བྱུང་བདེ་བའི་ཞིང་། །ལྷུན་མཉམ་བྱང་ཆུབ་མཆོག་གི་ངང་ཉིད་དོ།

།ཆོས་དབྱིངས་རིན་པོ་ཆེའི་མཛོད་ལས། །སྣང་སྲིད་ཞིང་ཁམས་སུ་ཤར་བའི་ལེའུ་སྟེ་གཉིས་པའོ།།

།།ཐམས་ཅད་ཀུན་འདུས་བྱང་ཆུབ་སེམས་སུ་འདུས། །བྱང་ཆུབ་སེམས་ལས་མ་གཏོགས་ཆོས་མེད་པས། །ཆོས་ཀུན་བྱང་ཆུབ་སེམས་ཀྱི་རང་བཞིན་ནོ།

།བྱང་ཆུབ་སེམས་ཀྱི་མཚོན་དཔེ་ནམ་མཁའ་འདྲ། །སེམས་ལ་རྒྱུ་མེད་སྐྱེ་བའི་ཡུལ་མེད་པས། །མི་གནས་བརྗོད་འདས་བསམ་ཡུལ་འདས་པ་ཉིད།། ནམ་མཁའི་དབྱིངས་ཞེས་དཔེ་རུ་མཚོན་པ་ཙམ། །མཚོན་དཔེ་ཉིད་ཀྱང་འདི་ཞེས་བྱར་མེད་ན། །མཚོན་དཔེའི་དོན་ལ་བསམ་བརྗོད་ག་ལ་སྲིད། ། འདི་ནི་རང་བཞིན་དག་པའི་དཔེར་ཤེས་བྱ།

It has no substance to delimit it and is free of the phenomena
of samsara and nirvana.
It cannot be characterized as some "thing," and being an
infinitely spacious expanse,
it is unchanging, without transition, spontaneously present,
and uncompounded.
Given that buddhahood lies within the vajra heart essence of
utter lucidity,
everything is a naturally occurring realm of bliss—
the very context of sublime enlightenment, a state of
spontaneous equalness.

This is the second section of *The Precious Treasury of the Basic Space of Phenomena,* concerning the universe of appearances and possibilities arising as a pure realm.

❖

EVERYTHING IS SUBSUMED within all-inclusive awakened
mind.
Since there is no phenomenon that is not included in awakened
mind,
the true nature of all phenomena is that of awakened mind.

Space is a metaphor for awakened mind.
Since that mind has no cause and is not an object that comes
into being,
it does not abide in any finite way, is inexpressible, and
transcends the realm of the imagination.
The phrase "the realm of space" is simply a way of illustrating
it metaphorically.
If even the metaphor itself cannot be described as some "thing,"
how could the underlying meaning that it illustrates be imagined
or described?
It should be understood as a metaphor for what is naturally
pure.

།དོན་ནི་རང་རིག་མཁའ་མཉམ་བྱང་ཆུབ་སེམས། །བསམ་པའི་ཡུལ་མིན་མཚོན་བརྗོད་འདས་པ་སྟེ། །རང་གསལ་མི་གཡོ་འོད་གསལ་ཡངས་པའི་ཀློང་། །མ་བྱས་ལྷུན་གྲུབ་ཡངས་དོག་མཐོ་དམན་མེད། །ཆོས་སྐུ་བྱང་ཆུབ་སྙིང་པོའི་དཀྱིལ་ཡངས་སོ།

།རྟགས་ནི་རྩལ་ལས་ཅིར་ཡང་འཆར་བ་སྟེ། །ཤར་བའི་དུས་ན་ཤར་ས་ཤར་མཁན་མེད། །ཤར་ཞིང་མེད་ཅམ་དཔྱད་ན་ནམ་མཁའ་འདྲ། །རིས་མེད་མཉམ་པ་ཆེན་པོར་ཧུབ་ཆུབ་པས། །ཕྱམ་གདལ་གཟུང་འཛིན་མེད་པའི་ཀློང་ཉིད་དོ།

།རང་བྱུང་ཡེ་ཤེས་ཆོས་ཉིད་ཕྱོགས་ཡན་ལ། །དཔེ་དོན་རྟགས་ཀྱི་ངེས་པའི་མཚོན་དཔེ་བསྟན། །མཁའ་མཉམ་གཟེར་ཆེན་གསུམ་གྱི་བདག་ཉིད་དུ། །ཐམས་ཅད་ཀུན་འདུས་རང་བཞིན་དབྱེ་བསལ་མེད། །ཕྱམ་མཉམ་ཡངས་པ་ཆེན་པོའི་དབྱིངས་རུམ་ན། །ཐམས་ཅད་ཡེ་མཉམ་སྤུ་ཕྱི་བཟང་ངན་མེད། །ཀུན་བཟང་རྡོ་རྗེ་སེམས་དཔའི་དགོངས་པའོ།

།བྱང་ཆུབ་སེམས་ནི་ཉི་མའི་སྙིང་པོ་འདྲ། །ངང་གིས་འོད་གསལ་ཡེ་ནས་འདུས་མ་བྱས། །

The underlying meaning is that awakened mind is self-knowing
awareness equal to space.
It is not within the realm of the imagination, for it defies
illustration or description.
Naturally lucid and unwavering, the spacious expanse of
utter lucidity
is not created but is spontaneously present, with no fixed reach
or range.
Dharmakaya is the spacious domain that is the heart essence
of enlightenment.

The evidence is that anything can and does arise due to the
dynamic energy of awareness.
Even as it arises, there is no place of arising or anything arising.
"Arising" is simply a label, for if examined, it is found to be
like space.
Everything being encompassed within a supreme state of
equalness without bias
constitutes the expanse of infinite evenness, which entails no
dualistic perception.

Given that naturally occurring timeless awareness—the true
nature of phenomena—is boundless,
analogies are used so that it can be ascertained through
metaphor, underlying meaning, and evidence.
Equal to space, that nature, which subsumes everything and
is without differentiation or exclusion,
is exemplified by these three linking factors.
In the womb of basic space, a supremely spacious state of
equalness,
everything is timelessly equal, with no time frame of earlier
or later, no better or worse.
This is the enlightened intent of Samantabhadra, of Vajrasattva.

Awakened mind can be compared to the sun.
It is utterly lucid by nature and forever uncompounded.

སྒྲིབ་པའི་ཆོས་མེད་ཟང་ཐལ་ལྷུན་གྱིས་གྲུབ། །སྤྲོས་པའི་ཆོས་མེད་མི་
རྟོག་ཆོས་ཉིད་དང་།

།སྟོང་པས་ཆོས་སྐུ་གསལ་བས་ལོངས་སྤྱོད་རྫོགས། །ཟེར་ལྡན་སྤྲུལ་པ་
སྐུ་གསུམ་འདུ་འབྲལ་མེད། །ཡེ་ནས་ཡོན་ཏན་ལྷུན་གྱིས་གྲུབ་ཟིན་པས།།
སྐྱོན་དང་ཉེས་ཆའི་མུན་པས་བསྒྲིབས་པ་མེད། །སྔ་ཕྱི་དུས་གསུམ་འཕོ་
འགྱུར་མེད་པར་གཅིག །སངས་རྒྱས་སེམས་ཅན་ཀུན་ལ་ཁྱབ་པར་གཅིག།
འདི་ནི་རང་བྱུང་བྱང་ཆུབ་སེམས་ཞེས་བྱ།

།དེ་ཡི་རྩལ་ནི་ཅིར་ཡང་འཆར་བ་སྟེ། །རྟོགས་དང་མི་རྟོགས་སྣང་སྲིད་
སྣོད་བཅུད་དང་། །སྐྱེ་འགྲོའི་སྣང་བ་སྣ་ཚོགས་ཇི་སྙེད་དོ།

།འདི་ཀུན་ཤར་ཡང་རང་བཞིན་འགག་མེད་དེ། །སྨིག་རྒྱུའི་ཆུ་དང་རྨི་
ལམ་སྒྲ་བརྙན་བཞིན། །སྤྲུལ་པ་གཟུགས་བརྙན་དྲི་ཟའི་གྲོང་ཁྱེར་དང་།
།མིག་ཡོར་ཇི་བཞིན་མེད་པ་གསལ་སྣང་དུ། །གཞི་མེད་རྟེན་མེད་གློ་བུར་
སྣང་བ་ཙམ། །བར་སྐབས་རེ་འགའི་ཆོས་སུ་རྟོགས་པར་བྱ།

།ལྷུན་གྲུབ་བྱང་ཆུབ་སེམས་ཀྱི་རང་བཞིན་ལས། །རོལ་པ་མ་འགགས་
འཁོར་འདས་ཆོ་འཕྲུལ་འབྱུང་། །ཆོ་འཕྲུལ་དེ་ཀུན་དབྱིངས་སུ་འུབ་
ཆུབ་པས།

།

With nothing to obscure it, it is unobstructed and
spontaneously present.
Without elaboration, it is the scope of the true nature
of phenomena, which does not entail concepts.

In being empty it is dharmakaya, in being lucid it is
sambhogakaya, and in being radiant it is nirmanakaya.
The three kayas do not come together or separate.
Since these enlightened qualities are already and forever
spontaneously present,
they are not obscured by the darkness of flaws and faults.
They are identical in being without transition or change
throughout the three times,
identical in permeating all buddhas and ordinary beings alike.
This is called "naturally occurring awakened mind."

Its dynamic energy arises as anything at all—
whether there is realization or not, there is the universe of
appearances and possibilities
and beings' perceptions in all their variety.

Though things arise, none of them has any independent
nature whatsoever.
Like water in a mirage, a dream, an echo,
a phantom emanation, a reflection, a castle in the air,
or a hallucination, all things are clearly apparent yet do not
truly exist—
they merely manifest adventitiously, without basis or support.
You should realize that all these manifestations are temporary,
adventitious phenomena.

Due to the nature of spontaneously present awakened mind,
there is a continuous display, the magical illusion of samsara
and nirvana.
Since this entire magical display is fully encompassed within
basic space,

གདོད་མའི་དང་ལས་གཡོས་པ་མེད་ཞེས་བྱ།

།འདིར་ནི་ཐམས་ཅད་བྱང་ཆུབ་སེམས་ཀྱི་དང་། །གཅིག་རྫོགས་ཀུན་རྫོགས་མ་བྱས་དོན་ཀུན་རྫོགས། །རང་བཞིན་ལྷུན་རྫོགས་རང་བྱུང་ཡེ་ཤེས་སོ།

།བྱང་ཆུབ་སེམས་ནི་སྣང་དང་མི་སྣང་ལས། །འཁོར་འདས་ཕྱི་ནང་ཆོས་སུ་མེད་ན་ཡང་། །དེ་ཡི་རྩལ་ལས་གཡོས་པའི་རང་བཞིན་གྱིས། །སྣང་སྲིད་འཁོར་འདས་སྣ་ཚོགས་རོལ་པར་ཤར།

།ཤར་ཙམ་ཉིད་ནས་རང་བཞིན་སྟོང་པའི་གཟུགས། །སྐྱེ་བ་མེད་ལས་སྐྱེ་བར་སྣང་བ་སྟེ། །སྣང་དུས་ཉིད་ནས་སྐྱེས་པ་འགའ་ཡང་མེད། །འགག་པ་མེད་ལས་འགག་པར་སྣང་ན་ཡང་། །འགག་པ་མེད་དེ་སྒྱུ་མ་སྟོང་པའི་གཟུགས། །གནས་པ་ཉིད་ནས་གནས་འི་ཆོས་མེད་དེ། །གནས་མཁན་གཞི་མེད་འགྲོ་འོང་མེད་པའི་དང་། །ཇི་ལྟར་སྣང་བ་དེ་ལྟར་མ་གྲུབ་པས། །རང་བཞིན་མེད་ཅེས་བཏགས་པ་ཙམ་དུ་ཟད།

།སྣང་བ་དེ་ཡང་རྩལ་ལས་རང་ཤར་བས། །རྟེན་འབྲེལ་ཉིད་ཅེས་རང་བཞིན་བརྡ་ཙམ་བརྗོད།

།

you should know that it does not stray from the scope of
primordial being.

Within this, everything is the scope of awakened mind.
With that single perfection, all is perfect—without being made
so, everything is perfect.
Naturally occurring timeless awareness is by nature
spontaneously perfect.

Given that awakened mind is neither apparent nor not apparent,
the outer and inner worlds of samsara and nirvana do
not exist as phenomena
yet arise nonetheless as a myriad display—
the universe of appearances and possibilities, whether of samsara
or nirvana—
because they are, by nature, the stirring of mind's dynamic
energy.

In simply arising, forms are by nature empty.
From what is unborn there manifests what seems to be born,
but even as it manifests, nothing whatsoever has been born.
From what is unceasing there manifests what seems to cease,
but there is no cessation.
These are illusory expressions of emptiness.
Even with abiding there is nothing that abides.
There is no basis on which anything could abide.
Within the context in which there is no coming or going,
regardless of what manifests, it never exists as what it
seems to be,
and so one is reduced to merely labeling it as "having no
independent nature."

Sensory appearances, moreover, arise naturally due to the
dynamic energy of awareness,
and so their nature is described in a purely symbolic way as
one of "interdependent connection."

རྩལ་ལས་ཤར་བར་སྣང་བའི་རང་དུས་ནས། །ཤར་དང་མ་ཤར་ཕྱོགས་དང་རིས་མེད་པས། །རྩལ་ཡང་བརྡ་ཙམ་ངོ་བོ་འགག་མེད་པས། །ཐམས་ཅད་རྟག་ཏུ་འཕོ་འགྱུར་མེད་པའི་ངང་། །བྱང་ཆུབ་སེམས་ལས་གཡོས་པ་རྡུལ་ཙམ་མེད།

།ཆོས་དབྱིངས་རིན་པོ་ཆེའི་མཛོད་ལས། །བྱང་ཆུབ་སེམས་ཀྱི་མཚོན་དཔེ་བསྟན་པའི་ལེའུ་སྟེ་གསུམ་པའོ།།

།།ཀུན་འདུས་བྱང་ཆུབ་སེམས་ཀྱི་རང་བཞིན་ནི། །སྣང་བ་མ་ཡིན་སྣང་བའི་ཆོས་ལས་འདས། །སྟོང་པ་མ་ཡིན་སྟོང་པའི་ཆོས་ལས་འདས། །ཡོད་པ་མ་ཡིན་དངོས་པོ་མཚན་མ་མེད། །མེད་པ་མ་ཡིན་འཁོར་འདས་ཀུན་ལ་ཁྱབ། །ཡོད་མེད་མ་ཡིན་ལྷུན་མཉམ་གདོད་མའི་དབྱིངས། །ཕྱོགས་དང་རིས་མེད་གཞི་རྩ་དངོས་པོ་མེད།

།རྒྱུན་ཆད་མེད་པས་རིག་པ་བྱང་ཆུབ་ཀློང་། །འཕོ་དང་འགྱུར་མེད་མཁའ་དབྱིངས་ཡེ་ནས་གདལ། །རང་བྱུང་ཡེ་ཤེས་དཔེ་ཟླ་མེད་པའི་དོན། །མི་སྐྱེ་མི་འགག་ཐིག་ལེ་གཅིག་ཏུ་འདུས། །མ་ངེས་ཀུན་ཁྱབ་ཕྱོགས་མཐའ་ཡོངས་ཀྱི་མེད།

Even in the very moment that things seem to arise due to that dynamic energy,
they do so without being subject to extremes or divisions—
with no question of whether or not something arises—
and even "dynamic energy" is just a symbolic term, with no finite essence whatsoever.
So within the context that is never subject to transition or change,
nothing strays in the slightest from awakened mind.

This is the third section of *The Precious Treasury of the Basic Space of Phenomena,* presenting the metaphors for awakened mind.

❖

It is the nature of all-inclusive awakened mind that it is not apparent,
for it transcends that which is apparent.
It is not empty, for it transcends that which is empty.
It is not existent, for it has no substance or characteristics.
Nor is it nonexistent, for it permeates all samsara and nirvana.
Neither existent nor nonexistent, it is primordial basic space, spontaneous and uniform,
not subject to extremes or division, and without substance, foundation, or underlying basis.

Uninterrupted, awareness is the expanse of awakened mind.
Without transition or change, the "sky" of basic space is timelessly and infinitely extensive.
Naturally occurring timeless awareness,
which has ultimate meaning in that nothing compares to it,
is subsumed within the single sphere of being, unborn and unceasing.
Indeterminate and all-pervasive, it is absolutely without limiting extremes.

།ལྷུན་མཉམ་མི་གཡོ་རྡོ་རྗེ་སྙིང་པོའི་གདུང་། །འདུ་འབྲལ་མེད་པའི་དབྱིངས་མཆོག་རབ་འབྱམས་འདི། །ཚིག་གིས་མཚོན་པའི་སྤྱོད་ཡུལ་མ་ཡིན་དེ། །ཤེས་རབ་ཀློང་རྡོལ་སོ་སོ་རང་རིག་ཡུལ། །བསམ་བརྗོད་སྤྲོས་དང་བྲལ་བའི་རྣལ་འབྱོར་པས། །མཚོན་དང་མི་མཚོན་མེད་པར་ཐག་བཅད་དེ། །སྒོམ་དང་བསྒོམ་པར་བྱ་བ་མ་རྙེད་པས། །བྱིང་རྒོད་རྣམ་རྟོག་དགྲ་བོ་བསད་མ་དགོས།

།ཡེ་ནས་སྤྱི་བླུགས་གནས་པའི་ཆོས་ཉིད་ལ། །བདག་དང་གཞན་དུ་རྟོག་པ་མི་མངའ་བས། །ཁམས་གསུམ་འདི་ཉིད་རང་བཞིན་མཉམ་པའི་ཞིང་།

།དུས་གསུམ་རྒྱལ་བ་རང་སྣང་དག་པ་སྟེ། །སྤང་བླང་མེད་པར་ཐམས་ཅད་ཕྱམ་གཅིག་པས། །གཞན་ནས་ཐོབ་པར་བྱ་བ་རྡུལ་ཙམ་མེད། །ཆོས་ཀུན་སེམས་ཉིད་ཀློང་ཆེན་དེར་གསལ་ལ། །མཉམ་པའི་དོན་ལས་གཡོས་པ་ཙུང་ཟད་མེད།

།ཕྱི་དང་ནང་མེད་འཆར་ནུབ་རྟོག་པ་མེད། །མཐའ་ཡི་མུན་སེལ་རྩ་བ་བྱང་ཆུབ་སེམས། །གང་ཡང་མ་སྤངས་གོལ་ས་ཤུགས་ལ་ཆོད།

The legacy of the vajra heart essence is one of unwavering
spontaneity and equalness.
The immensity of sublime basic space, which is not made
or unmade,
is not some finite range that can be characterized with words.
It is the welling forth of an expanse of sublime knowing, the
scope of one's self-knowing awareness.
A yogin who is free of conceptual and descriptive elaborations
comes to a decision that whether it can be characterized or not
is irrelevant.
Since neither meditation nor anything to meditate on can be
discovered,
there is no need to "slay the enemies" of dullness, agitation,
and thought.

Within the timelessly abiding, omnipresent state—the true
nature of phenomena—
there are no concepts of self or other,
and so the three realms themselves constitute a pure realm of
natural equalness.

For victorious ones of the three times, awareness's own
manifestations are pure.
Since everything constitutes a single state of equalness, with
nothing to renounce or accept,
there is nothing in the slightest to attain elsewhere.
All phenomena are clearly evident within the vast expanse of
mind itself,
yet they do not stray in the least from the ultimate meaning
of equalness.

There is no division into outer and inner, and no disturbance due
to thoughts arising and subsiding.
The foundation, awakened mind, dispels the darkness of
extremes.
With nothing having to be renounced, the potential for error is
cut through as a matter of course.

།འགྲོ་བའི་སྣང་ཚུལ་སྣ་ཚོགས་འཛིག་རྟེན་དང་། །དག་པའི་སངས་རྒྱས་སྐུ་དང་ཡེ་ཤེས་ཀྱང་། །རྟོགས་དང་མ་རྟོགས་རྩལ་ལས་ཤར་བ་ཡི། །རོལ་པ་མ་འགགས་ནམ་མཁའི་དབྱིངས་ཁྱབ་ཀུན། །ཆོས་དབྱིངས་ངང་ལ་རྟོགས་དང་མ་རྟོགས་ཙམ། །རྟོགས་པས་བདེ་གཤེགས་དག་པའི་སྣང་བ་དང་། །མ་རྟོགས་མ་རིག་གཟུང་འཛིན་བག་ཆགས་ལས། །སྣ་ཚོགས་སྣང་ཡང་དབྱིངས་ལས་གཡོས་པ་མེད།

།བྱང་ཆུབ་སེམས་ནི་ཀུན་གྱི་དངོས་གཞི་སྟེ། །མཚན་ཉིད་མ་འགགས་སྣ་ཚོགས་ཅིར་ཤར་ཡང་། །རང་གསལ་ཆོས་ཉིད་དག་པའི་དབྱིངས་སུ་གསལ། །དབྱེ་བསལ་མེད་དོ་རྒྱ་ཡན་རིག་པའི་འགྲོས།

།ཟང་ཐལ་ཡེ་ཤེས་རང་བྱུང་ཀློང་ཡངས་ཤིང་། །མ་བསྒྲིབས་ཕྱི་ནང་མེད་པར་འོད་གསལ་བས། །རང་རིག་སེམས་ཀྱི་མེ་ལོང་འོད་པོ་ཆེ། །འདོད་འབྱུང་ནོར་བུ་རིན་ཆེན་ཆོས་ཀྱི་དབྱིངས། །བཙལ་བ་མེད་པ་ཐམས་ཅད་རང་བྱུང་བས། །རང་བྱུང་ཡེ་ཤེས་འདོད་དགུར་འབྱུང་བའི་དཔལ།

The world of myriad ways in which beings perceive—
and even the kayas and timeless awareness of pure
buddhahood—
all that permeates the realm of basic space as a continuous
display
arises due to dynamic energy, either in light of realization or
in its absence.
There is simply realization or its lack within the realm of the
basic space of phenomena.
For those with realization, who have reached a state of bliss,
there is pure perception.
For those without it, there is nonrecognition of awareness and
the habitual patterns of dualistic perception,
from which sensory appearances manifest in all their variety,
though none of this strays from basic space.

Awakened mind is the actual state of everything.
It exhibits an unceasing quality.
Whatever arises in all its variety is naturally and clearly
apparent,
evident within pure basic space, the true nature of phenomena.
There is no division or exclusion—the mode of awareness is
without restriction.

Unobstructed timeless awareness, a naturally occurring spacious
expanse,
is utterly lucid—unobscured, with no division into outer and
inner—
and so self-knowing awareness is the great radiant mirror of
mind.
The precious gem that provides for all wants is the basic space
of phenomena.
Since everything occurs naturally without having to be sought,
naturally occurring timeless awareness is the splendid source of
all one could wish for.

།ཆེ་བའི་ཡོན་ཏན་རྣམ་གྲངས་ཇི་སྙེད་པ། །དབྱིངས་ལས་དབྱིངས་བྱུང་ཐབས་མཆོག་མ་འགགས་ཤར། །ཐམས་ཅད་སྐྱེ་མེད་དབྱིངས་སུ་ལྷུན་རྫོགས་པས། །དངོས་པོ་ཐྲེལ་གནོན་སྟོང་ཉིད་བྱང་ཆུབ་གླིང་། །སྟོང་པ་ཐྲེལ་གནོན་རང་རིག་བྱང་ཆུབ་གླིང་།

།བྱང་ཆུབ་སེམས་ལ་སྣང་སྟོང་ཡི་ནས་མེད། །གཉིས་མེད་མ་ཞེན་བསམ་ཡས་ཆོ་འཕྲུལ་འབྱུང་། །དུས་གསུམ་དུས་མེད་སྐྱེ་མེད་ཆོས་ཀྱི་དབྱིངས།། མི་འགྱུར་མི་ཕྱེད་འདུས་མ་བྱས་པའི་གླིང་། །དུས་གསུམ་སངས་རྒྱས་རིག་པའི་ཡེ་ཤེས་དབྱིངས། །གཟུང་འཛིན་ཐྲེལ་གནོན་རང་རིག་བྱང་ཆུབ་གླིང་། །ཕྱི་དང་ནང་མེད་ཆོས་ཉིད་ལྷུན་ཡངས་སོ།

།ཆོས་དབྱིངས་རིན་པོ་ཆེའི་མཛོད་ལས། །བྱང་ཆུབ་སེམས་ཀྱི་རང་བཞིན་བསྟན་པའི་ལེའུ་སྟེ་བཞི་པའོ།།

།།སེམས་ཉིད་བྱང་ཆུབ་སེམས་ཀྱི་ངོ་བོ་ལ། །ལྟ་བ་བསྒོམ་མེད་སྤྱོད་པ་སྤྱད་དུ་མེད། །འབྲས་བུ་བསྒྲུབ་མེད་ས་ལམ་བགྲོད་དུ་མེད། །དཀྱིལ་འཁོར་བསྐྱེད་མེད་བཟླས་བརྗོད་རྫོགས་རིམ་མེད། །དབང་ལ་བསྐུར་མེད་དམ་ཚིག་བསྲུང་དུ་མེད། །

However many great qualities can be enumerated,
they come from basic space and are of basic space, arising continuously as sublime skillful means.
Since everything is spontaneously perfect in unborn basic space,
the substance of things is outshone by their emptiness as the expanse of enlightenment,
while their emptiness is outshone by self-knowing awareness as the expanse of enlightenment.

In awakened mind, appearances and emptiness have never existed.
But do not fixate on nonduality, for the inconceivable miraculous display still occurs.
With no time frame, the unborn basic space of phenomena
is an unchanging, undivided, and uncompounded expanse.
Throughout the three times, buddhahood is awareness, the basic space of timeless awareness,
the expanse of enlightenment, of self-knowing awareness that outshines dualistic perceptions.
With no division into outer and inner, the true nature of phenomena is spontaneous and spacious.

This is the fourth section of *The Precious Treasury of the Basic Space of Phenomena,* demonstrating the nature of awakened mind.

❖

WITHIN MIND ITSELF—the essence of awakened mind—
there is no view to cultivate in meditation, no conduct to undertake,
no fruition to achieve, no levels of realization or paths to traverse,
no mandala to visualize, no recitation, repetition, or stage of completion,
no empowerment to be bestowed, and no samaya to uphold.

ཡི་ནས་ལྷུན་གྲུབ་དག་པའི་ཆོས་ཉིད་ལ། །གློ་བུར་རིམ་རྩོལ་རྒྱུ་འབྲས་ཆོས་ལས་འདས།

།འདི་དག་བྱང་ཆུབ་སེམས་ཀྱི་ངོ་བོ་སྟེ། །ཉི་མ་སྤྲིན་དང་མུན་པས་མ་བསྒྲིབས་ལ། །གློ་བུར་མ་བྱུས་དབྱིངས་ན་དངང་གིས་གསལ།

།རྩོལ་ཞིང་སྒྲུབ་པའི་ཆོས་བཅུ་གང་བསྟན་པ། །རྩལ་ལས་གློ་བུར་འཁྲུལ་ངོར་གསུངས་པ་ཉིད། །རིམ་རྩོལ་དབང་པོའི་རིམ་པས་འཇུག་པའི་ཐབས།། ཨ་ཏི་ཡོ་ག་རྡོ་རྗེ་སྙིང་པོའི་དོན། །ཇི་བཞིན་རྣལ་དུ་འབྱོར་ལ་བསྟན་པ་མིན།

།རིམ་འཇུག་རྩོལ་བ་ཅན་གྱི་གང་ཟག་རྣམས། །ཆོས་ཉིད་གདོད་མའི་དབྱིངས་སུ་དྲང་བའི་ཕྱིར། །ཉན་ཐོས་རང་རྒྱལ་བྱང་ཆུབ་སེམས་དཔའི་ཐེག །ཆུང་དུ་གསུམ་ལ་བསྟན་པའི་རིམ་པ་སྟེ། །ཀྲི་ཡ་ཨུ་པ་ཡོ་ག་རྣམ་པ་གསུམ། །འབྲིང་པོ་གསུམ་ལ་རང་བཞིན་བབས་ཀྱིས་གྲུབ།

།མ་ཧཱ་ཨ་ནུ་ཨ་ཏི་རྣམ་པ་གསུམ། །ཆེན་པོ་གསུམ་ལ་གདོད་ནས་སྣང་བ་སྟེ། །རྒྱུ་འབྲས་ཐེག་པའི་ཆོས་ཀྱི་སྒོ་དབྱེ་བས། །སྐལ་ལྡན་འགྲོ་བ་བྱང་ཆུབ་གསུམ་ལ་འདྲེན།

།ཀུན་ཀྱང་མཐར་ཐུག་རྡོ་རྗེ་སྙིང་པོའི་དོན། །

In the pure state that is the true nature of phenomena, timelessly
and spontaneously present,
such adventitious factors of developmental effort and causality
are transcended.

The essence of these factors is awakened mind.
Unobscured by clouds or darkness, the sun shines in the sky
by its very nature,
not as something adventitious.

Any teaching concerning the ten attributes that involve effort
and achievement
is given in response to the confusion that occurs adventitiously
due to the dynamic energy of awareness.
It is a skillful means for engaging those whose acumen requires
development through effort.
It is not given to yogins who genuinely experience
the ultimate meaning of the vajra heart essence, atiyoga.

So that individuals who exert themselves in order to progress
developmentally
may be led to primordial basic space—the true nature of
phenomena—
there are the spiritual approaches of the shravaka, the
pratyekabuddha, and the bodhisattva.
These are the stages demonstrated on the three lesser levels.
The three divisions of kriya, upa, and yoga
are by their very nature the three intermediate levels.

The three divisions of maha, anu, and ati
manifest primordially as the three higher levels.
By opening the doorway that leads beyond other approaches
based on causes or results,
they guide fortunate beings to three levels of enlightenment.

The culmination of all these, moreover, is found in the ultimate
meaning of the vajra heart essence.

གསང་ཆེན་སྨད་དུ་བྱུང་འདིར་འཇུག་དགོས་པས། །ཀུན་གྱི་རྩེ་མོ་འོད་གསལ་མཆོག་མི་འགྱུར། །མངོན་པར་བྱང་ཆུབ་སྙིང་པོའི་ཐེག་པར་གྲགས།

།ཆོས་ཀྱང་གཉིས་ལས་སྣང་དོར་བྱ་རྩོལ་ཅན། །རྩལ་ལས་རོལ་པར་ཤར་བའི་རང་བཞིན་གྱི། །སེམས་དང་སེམས་བྱུང་བག་ཆགས་སྦྱང་ཕྱིར་བསྟན། །དེ་དག་སེམས་ལས་ཡེ་ཤེས་དག་པར་འདོད།

།སྣང་དོར་བྱ་རྩོལ་མེད་པའི་ཆོས་ཆེན་ནི། །རང་བྱུང་ཡེ་ཤེས་བྱང་ཆུབ་སེམས་ཉིད་ཀྱི། །ངོ་བོ་ཐད་དྲང་ངང་ལས་མ་གཡོས་པར། །མངོན་དུ་བྱེད་པས་གཞན་དུ་རྩོལ་མི་དགོས། །རང་ལ་བཞག་ནས་གཞན་དུ་འཚོལ་མི་བྱེད།

།འདི་ནི་ཉི་མའི་ངོ་བོ་དེ་ཉིད་དོན། །རང་གཞག་འོད་གསལ་མི་གཡོ་གནས་པར་འདོད། །གཞན་ནི་སྒྲིབ་དང་སྨུན་སེལ་རྩོལ་སྒྲུབ་ཀྱིས། །ཉི་མ་གསར་སྒྲུབ་བྱེད་དང་མཚུངས་པར་བསྟན། །དེས་ན་འདི་གཉིས་ཁྱད་པར་གནམ་ས་བཞིན།

།དེང་སང་ཨ་ཏི་རློམ་པའི་གླང་ཆེན་དག །

They must lead toward this superb, supreme secret,
and so utter lucidity, sublimely unchanging, is the pinnacle of them all.
This is renowned as the spiritual approach of the heart essence of manifest enlightenment.

Furthermore, of the two alternatives within spiritual teaching,
one involves a concerted effort to accept or reject.
It is taught in order to refine away the habitual patterns of ordinary mind and mental events,
whose nature it is to arise as a display due to dynamic energy.
This approach holds that timeless awareness is purer than ordinary mind.

The supreme teaching involves no concerted effort to accept or reject.
Naturally occurring timeless awareness, the essence of awakened mind itself,
is made fully evident in that one does not waver from the direct experience of it.
So there is no need to strive for it elsewhere.
It rests in and of itself, so do not seek it elsewhere.

This—the ultimate meaning of suchness itself—is like the essence of the sun.
I hold that it abides as a natural state of rest, unwavering utter lucidity.
It can be shown that other approaches are like attempts to create the already-present sun
by dispelling clouds and darkness through a process of effort and achievement.
Therefore, these two kinds of approach are as different as heaven and earth.

Nowadays, those "elephants" who pride themselves on being ati practitioners

འགྱུ་འཕྲོའི་རྟོག་ཚོགས་བྱང་ཆུབ་སེམས་ཡིན་ལོ། །རྨོངས་པ་འདི་ཀུན་སྨུན་པའི་ཀློང་ཉིད་དང་། །རང་བཞིན་རྫོགས་པ་ཆེན་པོའི་དོན་ལ་རིང་།། རྩལ་དང་རྩལ་ལས་ཤར་བའང་མི་ཤེས་ན། །བྱང་ཆུབ་སེམས་ཀྱི་ངོ་བོ་སྨྲོས་ཅི་དགོས།

།འདིར་ནི་གདོད་ནས་དག་པའི་བྱང་ཆུབ་སེམས། །དོན་དམ་དབྱིངས་ཀྱི་ཆོས་ཉིད་བདེན་པ་ནི། །སྨྲ་བསམ་འདས་པས་ཤེས་རབ་ཕ་རོལ་ཕྱིན། །ངང་གིས་མི་གཡོ་རང་བཞིན་འོད་གསལ་ཞིང་། །འགྱུ་འཕྲོའི་སྤྲོས་དང་ཡེ་ནས་བྲལ་བ་ལ། །ངོ་བོ་ཞེས་བརྗོད་ཉི་མའི་སྙིང་པོ་འདྲ། །དེ་ཡི་རྩལ་ནི་འཆར་ཚུལ་མ་འགགས་པའི། །རིག་པ་ཟང་ཐལ་རྟོག་དཔྱོད་གཉིས་དང་བྲལ། །སལ་གྱིས་གསལ་ཡང་གཟུང་འཛིན་མེད་པ་ཡིན།

།རྩལ་ལས་ཤར་བའི་རིག་པ་སྤྲོས་པའི་བློ། །དེས་བསྐྱེད་གཟུང་འཛིན་བག་ཆགས་སྣ་ཚོགས་ཅན། །ཡུལ་མེད་ཡུལ་དུ་གཟུང་བའི་ཡུལ་ལྔ་དང་། །བདག་མེད་བདག་ཏུ་འཛིན་པའི་ཉོན་མོངས་ལྔ། །ཕྱི་ནང་སྣོད་བཅུད་འཁྲུལ་སྣང་ཇི་སྙེད་དེ། །འཁོར་བར་སྣང་བ་རྩལ་ལས་ཡང་ཤར་བ། །མ་རྟོགས་ལོག་པར་གཟུང་བའི་སྣང་བ་ཉིད།

allege that thought patterns, stirring and proliferating,
are awakened mind.
All of these fools are submerged in darkness,
far from the meaning of natural great perfection.
They do not understand even dynamic energy or what arises
from that energy,
to say nothing of the essence of awakened mind.

In this discussion of mine, primordially pure awakened mind
is ultimate truth—the true nature of phenomena as basic space.
Beyond description or imagination, it is the perfection of
sublime knowing.
Inherently unwavering, it is utterly lucid by nature
and timelessly free of elaboration—of concepts stirring and
proliferating—
and so is called "the essence of being," analogous to the orb
of the sun.
Its dynamic energy is unobstructed awareness as a continuous
mode for what arises
and is free of both conceptualization and analysis.
Though vividly lucid, it does not entail dualistic perception.

Awareness expresses itself through its dynamic energy as
consciousness that involves conceptual elaboration,
marked by the myriad dualistic habitual patterns that such
consciousness generates.
Since what are not objects are misconstrued as objects, there
are the five kinds of sense objects,
and since what has no identity is invested with identity, there
are the five afflictive emotions.
These constitute all possible confused perception—of the
universe and the beings within it.
Even what manifests as samsara arises due to that dynamic
energy,
but when this is not realized, the manifestation itself is one of
erroneous perception.

།གང་ནས་མ་འོངས་གང་དུ་མ་སོང་ལ། །གར་ཡང་མི་གནས་ཆོས་ཉིད་ཀློང་ཆེན་དུ། །རྟོགས་པས་ཁམས་གསུམ་ཡོངས་གྲོལ་དགོངས་པ་ཞེས། །ཨ་ཏི་ལྷུན་གྲུབ་རྡོ་རྗེ་སྙིང་པོའི་ལུང་། ཀུན་བཟང་ཡངས་པ་ཆེན་པོའི་ཀློང་ནས་ཤར།

།རྣམ་དག་བྱང་ཆུབ་སེམས་ཀྱི་ངོ་བོ་ལ། །ལྟ་བའི་ཡུལ་མེད་ལྟ་བའི་ཆོས་སུ་མེད། །བལྟ་བར་བྱ་དང་བྱེད་པ་རྡུལ་ཙམ་མེད། །སྒོམ་པའི་བློ་མེད་བསྒོམ་བྱའི་ཆོས་ཀུང་མེད། །སྤྱོད་དང་སྤྱོད་པ་གཉིས་མེད་ལྷུན་གྲུབ་པས།། བསྒྲུབ་པར་བྱ་བའི་འབྲས་བུ་རྡུལ་ཙམ་མེད།

།མེད་པའི་ཆོས་ལ་བགྲོད་པའི་ས་མེད་པས། །ཕྱིན་པར་བྱ་བའི་ལམ་ཡང་ཡི་ནས་མེད། །འོད་གསལ་ཐིག་ལེ་ཆེན་པོར་གྲུབ་ཟིན་པས། །རྣམ་རྟོག་འཕྲོ་འདུས་བསྐྱེད་པའི་དཀྱིལ་འཁོར་དང་། །སྔགས་དང་ཁ་དོན་དབང་དང་དམ་ཚིག་མེད། །རིམ་སྤྱད་ལ་སོགས་མི་དམིགས་རྫོགས་རིམ་མེད། །ཡི་ནས་གྲུབ་ཟིན་སྐུ་དང་ཡི་ཤེས་ལ། །འདུས་བྱས་བློ་བུར་རྐྱེན་བྱུང་རྒྱུ་འབྲས་མེད། །འདི་དག་ཡོད་ན་རང་བྱུང་ཡི་ཤེས་མིན། །

Through realization, within the vast expanse of being, of the
true nature of phenomena—
coming from nowhere, going nowhere, and abiding nowhere
at all—
there is "the enlightened intent of the total freedom of the
three realms."
This is the transmission of ati—spontaneous presence, the vajra
heart essence,
arising from the wholly positive expanse of supreme
spaciousness.

Within the essence of totally pure awakened mind,
there is no object to view or anything that constitutes a view—
not the slightest sense of anything to look at or anyone looking.
There is no ordinary consciousness meditating or anything to
meditate on.
Due to spontaneous presence, without any duality of goal and
conduct,
there is not the slightest sense of any fruition to achieve.

Regarding what is nonexistent, there are no levels of realization
to traverse,
and so there are never any paths to journey along.
Since utter lucidity is already ensured as the supreme sphere
of being,
there are no mandalas to visualize through the proliferation
and resolution of thoughts
and no mantras, recitations, empowerments, or samaya.
There is no nonreferential stage of completion, such as a gradual
process of dissolution.
In the kayas and timeless awareness, which are already ensured
timelessly,
there is no causality based on compounded adventitious
circumstances.
If any of these were the case, timeless awareness would not
occur naturally.

འདུས་བྱས་ཉིད་ཕྱིར་འཇིག་པ་ཉིད་དང་ནི། །ལྷུན་གྲུབ་འདུས་མ་བྱས་ཞེས་གང་སྨྲད་མཆོན།

།དེ་ཕྱིར་དོན་དམ་དབྱིངས་ཀྱི་ངོ་བོ་ལ། །རྒྱུ་འབྲས་ལས་འདས་རང་བཞིན་རྣམ་བཅུ་མེད། །རྩོལ་དང་སྒྲུབ་མེད་སེམས་ཉིད་རྣལ་མའི་དོན། །ཡོད་མེད་སྤྲོས་ཀུན་ཞི་བར་མཁྱེན་འཚལ་ལོ།

།ཆོས་དབྱིངས་རིན་པོ་ཆེའི་མཛོད་ལས། །རྩོལ་སྒྲུབ་རྒྱུ་འབྲས་ལས་འདས་པའི་ལེའུ་སྟེ་ལྔ་པའོ།།

།།ཉི་མའི་སྙིང་པོར་འོད་རྣམས་འདུས་པ་ལྟར། །ཆོས་ཀུན་རྩ་བ་བྱང་ཆུབ་སེམས་སུ་འདུས། །སྣང་སྲིད་སྣོད་བཅུད་མ་དག་འཁྲུལ་པ་ཡང་། །གང་བྱུང་རྟེན་དང་གནས་པའི་དབྱིངས་བརྟགས་པས། །གཞི་མེད་ཡེ་གྲོལ་སེམས་ཀྱི་ངང་དུ་འདུས། །ཆོས་ཉིད་ཡེ་གློང་ཡངས་པ་ཆེན་པོའི་ངང་། །འཁྲུལ་དང་མ་འཁྲུལ་མེད་དོན་འདས་པར་འདུས།

།དག་པའི་རང་སྣང་སྐུ་དང་ཞིང་ཁམས་དང་། །ཡེ་ཤེས་ཕྲིན་ལས་ངོ་མཚར་རོལ་པ་ཡང་། །

Being compounded, such awareness would be subject to
destruction,
and then how could it be characterized as "spontaneously
present and uncompounded"?

Therefore, within the essence of ultimate basic space,
causality is transcended and the ten attributes do not pertain.
Mind itself, the ultimate meaning of genuine being, involves no
effort or achievement.
Please understand this in order to pacify all conceptual
elaborations of existence and nonexistence!

This is the fifth section of *The Precious Treasury of the Basic Space of Phenomena,* demonstrating the transcendence of effort and achievement, cause and effect.

❖

JUST AS ALL LIGHT is subsumed within the sun as its source,
all phenomena are subsumed within awakened mind as their
source—
even the impurity and confusion in the universe of appearances
and possibilities.
Whatever occurs, by examining basic space as its matrix and
abode
you find that it has no foundation, but is subsumed within the
timeless freedom of mind.
Beyond labels and their meanings, confusion and its absence
are subsumed
within the true nature of phenomena—the timeless expanse,
a supremely spacious state.

Even the marvelous display of awareness's own pure
manifestations—
the kayas, pure realms, timeless awareness, and enlightened
activities—

རང་བྱུང་དང་ལ་འདུ་འབྲལ་མེད་པར་འདུས། །སྣང་སྲིད་འཁོར་འདས་ཀུན་འདུས་བྱང་ཆུབ་སེམས། །ཉི་མཁའ་བཞིན་དུ་སྟོང་གསལ་འདུས་མ་བྱས། །གདོད་ནས་རང་བྱུང་ཡེ་གློང་ཡངས་པ་ཡིན།

།སེམས་ཉིད་གློང་ཆེན་འགྱུར་མེད་ནམ་མཁའི་དང་། །རོལ་པ་ངེས་མེད་བྱང་ཆུབ་སེམས་ཀྱི་རྩལ། །འཁོར་འདས་ཐིག་པ་ཀུན་ལ་དབང་བསྒྱུར་བས། །བྱར་མེད་གཅིག་གིས་ཐམས་ཅད་ཐྲེལ་གྱིས་མནན། །མཐའ་རུ་གྱུར་པའི་ཡུལ་གཞན་ལོགས་ན་མེད། །ཆོས་ཉིད་བྱང་ཆུབ་སེམས་ལས་གར་མ་གཡོས།

།ཐམས་ཅད་ཀུན་བཟང་ལྷུན་གྲུབ་གཅིག་ཤར་བས། །མ་ལུས་ཀུན་འདུས་འགྲན་ཟླ་བྲལ་བའི་མཆོག །ཆེ་བའི་ཆེ་བ་ཀུན་བཟང་ཆོས་ཀྱི་དབྱིངས། །རྒྱལ་པོ་ལྟ་བུར་ཐམས་ཅད་ཀུན་འདུས་པས། །འཁོར་འདས་ཀུན་ལ་དབང་བསྒྱུར་གར་མ་གཡོས།

།ཐམས་ཅད་ཀུན་བཟང་མི་བཟང་གཅིག་མེད་པས། །བཟང་ངན་མེད་པར་ཀུན་ཏུ་བཟང་པོར་གཅིག །གྲུབ་དང་མ་གྲུབ་ཐམས་ཅད་དབྱིངས་གཅིག་པས།

།

is subsumed within the naturally occurring state that is not
made or unmade.
Awakened mind subsumes the universe of appearances and
possibilities, all of samsara and nirvana.
Lucid and uncompounded, it can be compared to the sun shining
in the empty sky.
Occurring primordially and naturally, it is a spacious, timeless
expanse.

Mind itself is an unchanging, vast expanse, the realm of space.
Its display, the dynamic energy of awakened mind, is
indeterminate.
In that it entails mastery over samsara, nirvana, and all spiritual
approaches,
this unique state, in which nothing need be done, outshines
everything else.
There is no context anywhere that constitutes an extreme.
There is no straying at all from the true nature of phenomena,
awakened mind.

Given that everything is wholly positive, arising as a single state
of spontaneous presence,
that which is sublime and without rival—
the greatest of the great, within which everything without
exception is subsumed—
is the wholly positive basic space of phenomena.
Since everything is united within it as though under a monarch,
it entails mastery over all samsara and nirvana and does not
waver at all.

Since everything is wholly positive, with not a single thing that is
not positive,
all things are identical within the wholly positive state, in which
there is neither good nor bad.
Since everything—whatever is or is not the case—is of the same
basic space,

ཐམས་ཅད་ལྷུན་གྲུབ་མི་གཡོ་མཉམ་པར་གཅིག

།གཅིག་ལས་ཀུན་ཤར་མ་ལུས་ཆོས་ཀྱི་དབྱིངས། །བྱར་མེད་ངང་ལ་སྒྲུབ་མེད་བཙལ་དུ་མེད། །རྩོལ་སྒྲུབ་རང་གི་དབྱིངས་ལས་གཞན་མེད་པས། །གང་ལས་རྩོལ་ཞིང་གང་དུ་སྒྲུབ་པར་བྱེད།

།བཙལ་བའི་ཡུལ་མེད་བསྒོམས་པས་མཐོང་བ་མེད། །བསྒྲུབ་པའི་གནས་མེད་གཞན་ནས་འོང་བ་མེད། །འགྲོ་འོང་མེད་པས་མཉམ་ཉིད་ཆོས་ཀྱི་སྐུ། །ལྷུན་རྫོགས་ཐིག་ལེ་ཆེན་པོའི་དབྱིངས་སུ་འདུས།

།ཉན་ཐོས་རང་རྒྱལ་བྱང་ཆུབ་སེམས་དཔའི་ལུགས། །བདག་དང་བདག་གི་མེད་པར་ཐག་བཅད་ནས། །སྤྲོས་བྲལ་ནམ་མཁའ་འདྲ་བར་དགོངས་དོན་གཅིག །ཨ་ཏི་མཆོག་གསང་རྣལ་འབྱོར་ཆེན་པོའི་ལུགས། །བདག་གཞན་དབྱེར་མེད་ཡངས་པའི་ནམ་མཁའ་ལ། །རང་བྱུང་ཡེ་ཤེས་ཇི་བཞིན་རྣལ་འཇོག་པས། །དགོངས་དོན་དེ་ཀུན་སྙིང་པོའི་མཆོག་འདིར་འདུས།

།ཀྲི་ཡ་ཨུ་པ་ཡོ་ག་རིགས་གསུམ་ཡང་། །བདག་དང་ལྷ་དང་ཏིང་འཛིན་མཆོད་སྤྲིན་ལས། །སྒོ་གསུམ་རྣམ་དག་དངོས་གྲུབ་འདོད་པར་གཅིག །

all things are identical within the unwavering, spontaneously
present state of equalness.

The single state from which everything without exception arises
is the basic space of phenomena.
There is nothing to achieve or to seek within the context in
which nothing need be done.
Since effort and achievement are not other than their natural
state of basic space,
whence could effort come? To what achievement could it lead?

Since there is no object to seek, nothing to perceive in
meditation,
no state to achieve, nothing that comes from anywhere else,
and no coming or going, there is equalness—dharmakaya.
This spontaneous perfection is found within the basic space of
the supreme sphere of being.

The transmissions of shravakas, pratyekabuddhas, and
bodhisattvas
are decisive concerning the nonexistence of both the self and
what pertains to it,
and so they are identical in their intent, a spacelike state free
of elaboration.
The transmission of supreme yoga—the sublime secret of ati—
is that of resting in genuine being, just as it is—naturally
occurring timeless awareness—
within the spacious state in which there is no distinction between
self and other.
So the ultimate meaning of the enlightened perspectives of all
three lower approaches
is subsumed within this sublime heart essence.

The three approaches of kriya, upa, and yoga, moreover,
which employ oneself, deity, meditative absorption, and clouds
of offerings,
are identical in holding that spiritual attainment comes from
the complete purification of body, speech, and mind.

རྡོ་རྗེ་རྩེ་མོ་ལྷུང་རྒྱལ་གསང་བ་ཡང་། །སྣང་གྲགས་རིག་པ་རྣམ་དག་ཡེ་ནས་ལྷ། །སྒོ་གསུམ་རྣམ་དག་དངོས་གྲུབ་མངོན་གྱུར་པས། །དགོངས་པ་དེ་ཀུན་སྙིང་པོའི་མཆོག་འདིར་འདུས།

།མ་ཧཱ་ཨ་ནུ་ཨ་ཏི་རིམ་གསུམ་ཡང་། །སྣང་སྲིད་སྣོད་བཅུད་ལྷ་དང་ལྷ་མོའི་ཞིང་། །དབྱིངས་དང་ཡེ་ཤེས་རྣམ་དག་དབྱེར་མེད་པས། །ཆོས་ཉིད་མི་གཡོ་རང་བྱུང་ཡེ་ཤེས་འདོད། །མཆོག་གསང་རབ་འདིར་ཐམས་ཅད་རྣམ་དག་པས། །མ་བྱས་གཞལ་ཡས་ཡེ་ཀློང་བདེ་བའི་ཞིང་། །ཕྱི་དང་ནང་མེད་ཀུན་ཁྱབ་གདལ་བ་ལས། །སྤང་དོར་བྱ་རྩོལ་མཚན་མའི་ཆོས་མེད་པར། །ཐམས་ཅད་ཡེ་འབྱམས་ཆོས་སྐུའི་ཀློང་ཡངས་པས། །དགོངས་པ་དེ་ཀུན་གསང་ཆེན་སྙིང་པོར་འདུས།

།གཅིག་རྫོགས་ཀུན་རྫོགས་ཆོས་ཀུན་འདུས་པའི་ཀློང་། །ཡེ་བབས་རང་གསལ་ལྷུན་གྲུབ་ཆེན་པོར་འདུས།

།ཆོས་དབྱིངས་རིན་པོ་ཆེའི་མཛོད་ལས། །ཐམས་ཅད་བྱང་ཆུབ་སེམས་སུ་འདུས་པར་བསྟན་པའི་ལེའུ་སྟེ་དྲུག་པའོ།།

However, according to the secret and most majestic transmission
of the vajra pinnacle,
appearances, sounds, and awareness are completely pure—
timelessly the deity.
Spiritual attainment is fully evident as the complete purity of
body, speech, and mind,
and so the enlightened perspectives of all these approaches are
subsumed within this sublime heart essence.

In the three stages of maha, anu, and ati, moreover,
the universe of appearances and possibilities is a pure realm of
masculine and feminine deities.
These stages hold that the unwavering nature of phenomena is
naturally occurring timeless awareness,
for basic space and timeless awareness are inseparable in their
total purity.
Given that everything is completely pure within this sublime,
excellent secret,
the immeasurable mansion, without being created, is a blissful
realm, a timeless expanse.
Within this infinite and all-pervasive state, which cannot be
divided into outer and inner,
there is nothing to characterize in light of your value judgments.
With everything timelessly infinite—the spacious expanse of
dharmakaya—
the enlightened perspectives of all these approaches are
subsumed within the heart essence of the supreme secret.

Perfection in one, perfection in everything—
the expanse within which all phenomena are subsumed
is itself subsumed within the supreme state of spontaneous
presence,
a timeless and naturally lucid state of utter relaxation.

This is the sixth section of *The Precious Treasury of the Basic Space of Phenomena,* demonstrating that everything is subsumed within awakened mind.

།།རང་བཞིན་ལྷུན་གྲུབ་བྱང་ཆུབ་སེམས་ཀྱི་ལུང་། །མ་བྱས་དོན་གྲུབ་རི་རྒྱལ་རྩེ་མོ་ནི། །ཀུན་ལས་འཕགས་སོ་ཐེག་མཆོག་རྒྱལ་པོ་ཆེ།

།ཇི་ལྟར་རི་རྒྱལ་རྩེ་མོར་ཕྱིན་པ་ན། །དམའ་བའི་ལུང་རྣམས་དུས་གཅིག་མཐོང་བ་སྟེ། །ལུང་གི་རྩེ་མོའི་རང་བཞིན་མཐོང་དང་བྲལ། །དེ་བཞིན་ཨ་ཏི་རྡོ་རྗེ་སྙིང་པོ་ནི། །ཐེག་པའི་ཡང་རྩེ་དོན་ཀུན་གསལ་བར་མཐོང་། །འོག་མའི་ཐེག་པས་འདི་དོན་མཐོང་བ་མེད། །དེ་ཕྱིར་ལྷུན་གྲུབ་རྩེ་མོར་གྱུར་པའི་རྩེ།

།ཇི་ལྟར་ཡིད་བཞིན་ནོར་བུ་ཆེན་པོ་ལ། །གསོལ་བ་བཏབ་ན་འདོད་དགུ་ངང་གིས་འབྱུང་། །ཕལ་པའི་དངོས་ལ་དེ་ལྟར་མ་ཡིན་ནོ། །རྡོ་རྗེ་སྙིང་པོ་སྐུ་གསུམ་ལྷུན་གྲུབ་པས། །རང་གཞག་དབྱིངས་ལས་སངས་རྒྱས་རང་ལ་འགྲུབ། །རྩོལ་ཞིང་སྒྲུབ་མེད་ཆེ་བ་དེ་ཉིད་དོ། །འོག་མའི་ཐེག་པས་བླང་དོར་འབད་བྱས་ཀྱང་། །བསྐལ་པར་མི་འགྲུབ་ཆི་ཆད་ནད་དུ་ཆེ།

།ཡེ་ནས་ལྷུན་མཉམ་རིག་པ་བྱང་ཆུབ་སེམས། །ཇི་བཞིན་རང་བབས་ཆོས་ཉིད་ཡངས་པ་ནི། །རང་བཞིན་ཆོས་སྐུ་མཉམ་ཉིད་གདོད་མའི་ཀློང་། །

THE TRANSMISSION of awakened mind, spontaneously present by nature,
is the summit of the most majestic mountain, not created yet ensuring all that has ultimate meaning.
Exalted above all, it is the supreme and most majestic spiritual approach.

Once one has reached the summit of a majestic mountain,
one can see the valleys below all at once,
while from the valleys one cannot see what it is like at the summit.
Similarly, ati, the vajra heart essence,
is the pinnacle spiritual approach and sees what is meaningful in all others,
while the lower approaches cannot see its ultimate meaning.
Therefore, it is the pinnacle, the peak experience, which is spontaneously present.

It is like a great wish-fulfilling gem that, if prayed to,
ensures all that is wished for as a matter of course.
Such is not the case for ordinary things.
Since the vajra heart essence is the spontaneous presence of the three kayas,
buddhahood is ensured, in and of itself, within the basic space of natural rest.
It does not require effort or achievement—that is its superiority.
Although those in lower approaches strive through acceptance and rejection,
they accomplish nothing for eons—what a great debility!

Awakened mind—timelessly spontaneous and uniform awareness—
the spacious nature of phenomena, just as it is, the naturally settled state,
is dharmakaya by nature, the expanse of primordial equalness.

ཀུན་ལ་ཡོད་དེ་སྐལ་ལྡན་འགའ་ཡི་ཡུལ། །ཇི་བཞིན་བཞག་ན་ངང་དེར་བབས་ཀྱིས་འགྱུབ།

།ཁྱབ་གདལ་རང་གསལ་ལྷུན་གྲུབ་ལོངས་སྤྱོད་རྫོགས། །ཀུན་ལ་ཡོད་ཀྱང་མཐོང་བ་འགའ་ཡི་ཡུལ། །གང་སྣང་རང་གཞག་བྱ་རྩོལ་བྲལ་ན་མངོན།

མ་འགགས་རོལ་པ་སྤྲུལ་སྐུ་གདལ་བའི་ཀློང་། །ཀུན་ལ་ཡོད་དེ་འཆར་བའི་དུས་ན་གསལ། །ཡིད་བཞིན་ཡོན་ཏན་ཕྲིན་ལས་ཚོ་འཕྲུལ་ཡང་། །གཞན་ན་མེད་དེ་རང་རིག་དག་པའི་ཀློང་། །ཆུ་དང་རློག་བཞིན་རང་དངས་བཞག་ན་གསལ།

།བཙལ་བས་མི་རྙེད་གདོད་ནས་དག་པའི་ཆོས། །སངས་རྒྱས་བྱང་ཆུབ་རང་བྱུང་ཀློང་ན་གསལ། །སྦྱར་གྲུབ་ཟིན་པས་ད་གཟོད་བསྒྲུབ་མི་དགོས།། ཆེ་བ་རང་གནས་དགོངས་པ་ཆོས་ཉིད་ཀློང་། །མི་འགྱུར་ལྷུན་གྱིས་གྲུབ་ལ་རྩོལ་མི་བྱེད།

།ཡི་གཞི་བབས་གཞི་བྱང་ཆུབ་སྙིང་པོའི་གཞི། །རང་བཞིན་ངང་ལས་གཡོས་པ་འགག་མེད་པས། །ཀློང་གསལ་རིག་པའི་དོན་ལས་མ་གཡོ་ཞིག

།ཐམས་ཅད་བཞག་པས་འགྲུབ་པའི་རྒྱུ་མཚན་ཡང་། །མི་འགྱུར་ཀུན་འགྲོ་ཁྱབ་བདག་ཡི་ཤེས་ལྷ། །

It is present in everyone but within the reach of only a fortunate few.
If left just as it is, it is innately ensured within that context.

Sambhogakaya—infinitely pervasive, naturally lucid, and spontaneously present—
is present in everyone, but the perception of it is within the reach of only a few.
If you rest naturally with whatever manifests, without conscious striving, it is evident.

The continuous display is the infinite expanse of nirmanakaya.
It is present in everything, clear in the arising of things.
It is the pure expanse of self-knowing awareness.
The miraculous display of wish-fulfilling qualities and activities, moreover, is nowhere else.
Like turbid water when the sediment settles, it becomes clear if you rest in the naturally pristine state.

The truth of primordial purity is not found by being sought.
Enlightenment—buddhahood—is evident within the naturally occurring expanse.
Since it has already been accomplished, there is no need to achieve it anew.
This naturally abiding greatness is enlightened intent, the expanse that is the true nature of phenomena.
Make no effort concerning what is unchanging and spontaneously present!

The timeless ground, the innately abiding ground, is the ground that is at the very heart of enlightenment.
Since it does not stray at all from the context that is its nature,
do not stray from the lucid expanse that is the ultimate meaning of awareness!

The reason that everything is ensured by being left as it is
lies in the unchanging, ever-present state of sovereign mastery—
the five aspects of timeless awareness.

སྐུ་ལྷ་གསུང་ལྷ་ཐུགས་ལྷ་ཡོན་ཏན་ལྷ། །ཕྲིན་ལས་ལྷ་སྟེ་དང་པོའི་སངས་རྒྱས་ཀྱང་། །ཐོག་མཐའ་མེད་པའི་ཀློང་འདིར་ལྷུན་གྲུབ་པས། །གཞན་དུ་མ་འཚོལ་རང་བཞིན་ཡེ་ནས་གྲུབ།

།སངས་རྒྱས་ཀུན་གྱི་ཆོས་སྐུ་བྱང་ཆུབ་ཀྱང་། །མི་འགྱུར་མཉམ་པའི་དོན་ལས་གཞན་དུ་མེད། །དེ་ཡང་རང་བྱུང་ངང་འདིར་ལྷུན་གྲུབ་པས། །མ་ཚོལ་མ་བསྒྲུབས་རེ་དོགས་ལྷུན་གྱིས་ཞོག

།སེམས་ཅན་ཀུན་གྱི་རང་བྱུང་ཡེ་ཤེས་ཀྱང་། །མ་བྱས་མ་བཅལ་ཆོས་སྐུར་ལྷུན་གྲུབ་པས། །སྤང་བླང་མ་འཛིན་ཆོས་དབྱིངས་ངང་འདིར་ཞོག

།མི་གཡོ་མི་བསམ་ལྷུན་མཉམ་ངོ་བོ་ལ། །མ་བྱས་དོན་གྲུབ་གཞི་ཀློང་ཡངས་པ་ཡིན།

།མི་འགྱུར་ཀུན་འགྲོ་སྐུ་དང་ཡེ་ཤེས་བདག །རྒྱལ་ཐབས་སྤྱི་བླུགས་རང་བྱུང་ཆེན་པོའི་དབང་། །སྣང་སྲིད་སྣོད་བཅུད་ཡེ་ནས་ལྷུན་གྲུབ་པས། །བྱ་རྩོལ་མི་དགོས་རང་བཞིན་ལྷུན་གྱིས་གྲུབ། །

The state of original buddhahood—the five aspects each of
enlightened form, enlightened speech, enlightened mind,
enlightened qualities, and enlightened activity—
is spontaneously present within the beginningless and endless
expanse.
Do not seek it elsewhere, for by nature it is timelessly ensured.

Moreover, enlightenment—dharmakaya as experienced by
all buddhas—
is none other than the ultimate meaning of unchanging
equalness.
And since it is spontaneously present within that naturally
occurring context,
do not seek it, do not try to achieve it.
Completely let go of hope and fear!

Even the naturally occurring timeless awareness of all
ordinary beings
is unmade and unsought, and spontaneously present as
dharmakaya,
so do not react with rejection or acceptance, but rest in this
context of basic space!

Within the essence of being—spontaneous and uniform,
unwavering and beyond deliberation—
lies the spacious expanse of the ground of being, not created
yet ensuring all that has ultimate meaning.

Unchanging and ever-present, the embodiment of the kayas
and timeless awareness
is the conferral of the supreme, naturally occurring
empowerment, like the investiture of a royal heir.
Since the universe of appearances and possibilities is timelessly
and spontaneously present,
there is no need for concerted effort, for it is spontaneously
present by nature.

ཐམས་ཅད་ཀུན་གྲུབ་ལྷུན་གྲུབ་ཆེན་པོར་རྒྱས།

།ཆོས་དབྱིངས་རིན་པོ་ཆེའི་མཛོད་ལས། །ཐམས་ཅད་བྱང་ཆུབ་ཀྱི་སེམས་
སུ་ཡི་ནས་ལྷུན་གྱིས་གྲུབ་པར་བསྟན་པའི་ལེའུ་སྟེ་བདུན་པའོ།།

།།ཐམས་ཅད་དབྱིངས་གཅིག་རང་བྱུང་ཡེ་ཤེས་ལ། །གཉིས་སུ་མེད་པ་ངོ་
བོའི་འདུག་ཚུལ་ཏེ། །གཉིས་སྣང་མ་འགགས་རྩལ་ལས་རོལ་པར་ཤར།།
སྣང་བཏགས་གཉིས་མེད་བྱང་ཆུབ་སེམས་ཞེས་བྱ།

།འཕོ་འགྱུར་མེད་པའི་རིག་པ་བྱང་ཆུབ་ལ། །སྤྱངས་ཐོབ་མེད་པའི་སྣང་
སྲིད་འཁོར་འདས་ཤར། །གཟུང་འཛིན་མེད་པའི་རྣལ་འབྱོར་ངོ་ཁ་ལ། །
མེད་ལ་སྣང་འདི་ཡ་མཚན་དགོད་པོ་འཚོར།

།སྣང་བར་མེད་ལ་སྣ་ཚོགས་སྣང་བར་ཤར། །སྟོང་པར་མེད་ལ་མཐའ་
དབུས་ཁྱབ་པར་གདལ། །གཟུང་འཛིན་མེད་ལ་ང་བདག་སོ་སོར་ཞེན། །
གཞི་རྩ་མེད་ལ་ཚེ་རབས་བརྒྱུད་མར་སྣང་། །

Everything is ensured, unfolding as a supreme state of
spontaneous presence.

This is the seventh section of *The Precious Treasury of the Basic Space of Phenomena,* demonstrating that everything is timelessly and spontaneously present within awakened mind.

❖

WITHIN NATURALLY OCCURRING timeless awareness, a single
basic space,
all things are present in such a way that they are in essence
nondual.
Continuous dualistic perceptions arise as a display due to the
dynamic energy of awareness.
In what is called "awakened mind," there is no duality of
sensory appearances and what the mind imputes about them.

Within enlightenment—awareness without transition or
change—
the universe of appearances and possibilities, whether of samsara
or nirvana,
arises with nothing to renounce or attain.
In the experience of yogins who do not perceive things
dualistically,
the fact that things manifest without truly existing is so amazing
they burst into laughter.

Although sensory appearances do not exist, they manifest
in all their variety.
Although emptiness does not exist, it extends infinitely,
reaching everywhere.
Although dualistic perception does not exist, there is still
fixation on things having individual identity.
Although they have no basis, a continual succession of lifetimes
manifests.

དགག་སྒྲུབ་མེད་ལ་བདེ་སྡུག་བླང་དོར་བྲེད།

།ཕར་བལྟས་སྐྲི་འགྲོའི་སྣང་བ་མཚར་རེ་ཆེ། །མི་བདེན་བདེན་པར་ཞེན་པས་བདེན་བདེན་འདྲ། །མ་འཁྲུལ་འཁྲུལ་པར་ཞེན་པས་འཁྲུལ་འཁྲུལ་འདྲ། །ངེས་མེད་ངེས་པར་བཟུང་བས་ངེས་ངེས་འདྲ། །ཡིན་མིན་ཡིན་པར་བཟུང་བས་ཡིན་ཡིན་འདྲ། །མི་འཐད་འཐད་པར་བཟུང་བས་འཐད་འཐད་འདྲ།

།སྣ་ཚོགས་ཅོལ་ཆུང་ཡུལ་གྱིས་སེམས་བྲིད་ནས། །དོན་མེད་རིག་པ་སྐད་ཅིག་བརྒྱུད་མར་མཐུད། །ཉིན་ཞག་ཟླ་བ་ལོ་དང་མི་ཚེ་འདས། །གཉིས་མེད་གཉིས་སུ་བཟུང་བས་འགྲོ་བ་བསླུས།

།རྣལ་འབྱོར་དག་པའི་སེམས་ལ་རྩར་བལྟས་པས། །རྟེན་གཞི་མེད་པའི་རིག་པ་མིང་དང་བྲལ། །མཚོན་བརྗོད་མ་མཐོང་ལྷ་སྒོམ་ཁྲིགས་ཆགས་བུད། །ཕྱལ་བ་ལྷུག་པ་ཡངས་པ་ཕྱམ་གདལ་བས། །ཉམས་ལེན་མ་ཤེས་ཐུན་མཚམས་ཕྱོགས་རིས་མེད། །ཐམས་ཅད་རྒྱ་ཡན་ཕྱམ་ཕྱམ་བར་མཚམས་བྲལ།

།ལུས་དང་ཡུལ་དང་སྣང་བའི་གདད་མེད་པར། །

Although nothing exists that can be refuted or proved, pleasure is accepted and pain is rejected.

Looking around, I find the perception of beings to be truly amazing.
They fixate on what is not real as real, so that it certainly seems real.
They fixate on confusion where there is no confusion, so that there certainly seems to be confusion.
They reify what is indeterminate as determinate, so that it certainly seems determinate.
They reify what is not so as being so, so that it certainly seems so.
They reify what is untenable as tenable, so that it certainly seems tenable.

Ordinary mind is seduced by trivial sense objects in all their variety.
One's useless focus moment by moment extends into a continuum,
as days, months, years, whole lives go by.
Beings are deceived by misconstruing what is not dualistic as dualistic.

As a yogin with a pure mind looks inward,
awareness, without underlying support or basis, is free of labels.
It cannot be perceived in any way that can be characterized or described—
structured view and meditation are done away with.
Given this state of infinite evenness, open, relaxed, and spacious,
there is no sense of spiritual practice, for there is no distinction between formal sessions and the periods in between.
Everything is unrestricted, completely equal, and uninterrupted.

With no reference point—whether body or sense object or perception—

ནམ་མཁའི་ཀློང་ཡངས་མཉམ་པར་ཕྲུམ་གདལ་བས། །ནང་གི་ཆོས་ཞེས་བདག་ཏུ་འཛིན་པ་མེད།

།ཕྱི་རོལ་སྣང་བའི་ཡུལ་ལ་ཕར་བལྟས་པས། །ཐམས་ཅད་སང་སེང་འལ་འོལ་ཟང་མ་ཐལ། །ར་རི་ཟབ་ཟེབ་གཟའ་གཏད་ཆོས་དང་བྲལ། །སྣང་གྲགས་དྲན་རིག་སྤྲོང་ཆོར་སྤུར་བཞིན་མེད། །འདི་ཅི་རང་བཞིན་སྤྲུན་པའི་སྣང་བའམ། །སྨི་ལམ་ནང་ཞེས་རང་ལ་དགོད་པོ་འཆོར།

།དགྲ་གཉེན་ཆགས་སྡང་ཉེ་རིང་འདུ་ཤེས་བྲལ། །ཉིན་མཚན་རིས་མེད་མཉམ་པར་ཕྲུམ་གཅིག་པས། །དམིགས་གཏད་མཚན་མར་འཛིན་པའི་འཁོར་བ་སངས། །རང་བྱུང་ཡེ་ཤེས་དང་ཞེས་མི་རྟོག་པས། །སླང་དོར་སྤང་གཉེན་གཟེབ་ལས་འདས་པ་ཡིན། །འདི་ལྟར་རྟོགས་ན་གཉིས་མེད་ཡེ་ཤེས་ཏེ། །རང་བྱུང་ཀུན་ཏུ་བཟང་པོའི་དགོངས་པར་ཕྱིན། །ལྷོག་པའི་གནས་མེད་ཟད་པའི་སར་ཕྱིན་ཏོ།

།རང་བྱུང་དང་ནས་མཉམ་ཉིད་མ་རྟོགས་པར། །གཉིས་མེད་ཉིད་ཅེས་ཚིག་ལ་མངོན་ཞེན་ནས། །ཅི་ཡང་མི་དམིགས་ཡིད་དཔྱོད་གདེང་འཆའ་བ། །ལོག་རྟོག་ཉིད་དེ་མ་རིག་མུན་པའི་ཀློང་།

there is infinite evenness within the undifferentiated, vast
expanse of space,
and so there is no inner agent that can be held to have identity.

As you look outward at sense objects manifesting externally,
everything is unobstructed, vivid yet ephemeral,
random, without any reference point.
You perceive, hear, think, are aware, experience, and feel
as never before.
"What is this? Are my perceptions by nature those of a lunatic?
Am I in a dream?"
You burst out laughing at yourself!

You are free of any notion of enemy or friend, attachment or
aversion, near or far.
Since there is a unique evenness in that everything is equal,
without any distinction between day and night,
samsara—the reifying of characteristics and reference points—
is cleared away.
Since you have no concepts about "the scope of naturally
occurring timeless awareness,"
you have transcended the cage of acceptance and rejection,
of what is an antidote and what is to be abandoned.
With such realization, there is nondual timeless awareness.
You have arrived at enlightened intent, naturally occurring
and wholly positive.
You have arrived at the point of resolution, with no chance
of falling back.

Without any realization of equalness in its naturally
occurring state,
you may obsess on the word "nonduality"
and place your confidence in some state that you speculate
has no frame of reference whatsoever.
This is truly a mistaken notion—the dark realm in which
awareness is not recognized.

།དེ་ཕྱིར་རང་བྱུང་འཕོ་འགྱུར་མེད་པ་ལ། །བསམ་རྫོགས་རྒྱལ་པོ་གཉིས་སུ་མེད་པར་སྤྲུང་། །ཁམས་གསུམ་ཡོངས་གྲོལ་འཁོར་འདས་གཉིས་མེད་དོན། །རང་བཞིན་ཁོང་ནས་རང་ཤར་ཆོས་སྐུའི་རྫོང་། །མཁའ་ལྟར་རྣམ་དག་དཔེ་ལས་འདས་པ་འབྱུང་།

།འདི་དང་འདི་ཞེས་སོ་སོར་ཞེན་པའི་བར། །གཉིས་སུ་གནས་པས་རང་གཞན་འཁྲུལ་པའི་གཟེབ། །གང་ཚེ་འདི་ཞེས་ཐ་དད་རིས་མེད་ཅིང་། །ཐམས་ཅད་ཕྱམ་མཉམ་དམིགས་གཏད་མེད་པ་ན། །གཉིས་མེད་རྟོགས་ཞེས་རྡོ་རྗེ་སེམས་དཔས་གསུངས།

།ཆོས་དབྱིངས་རིན་པོ་ཆེའི་མཛོད་ལས། །བྱང་ཆུབ་ཀྱི་སེམས་ལ་གཉིས་སུ་མེད་པར་བསྟན་པའི་ལེའུ་སྟེ་བརྒྱད་པའོ།།

།།རང་བཞིན་ཡངས་པ་ཆེན་པོའི་ཀློང་གཅིག་ལ། །མཁའ་མཉམ་བྱང་ཆུབ་སེམས་ཀྱི་གནམ་གཟེར་ནི། །གནད་དུ་དྲིལ་ཏེ་བཙུད་དུ་ཕྱུང་བ་ནི། །ཆེ་བའི་ཆེ་བ་ཀུན་བཟང་ཡངས་པའི་ཐུགས། །རང་གི་ངོ་བོས་སྤྱི་རྒྱ་རླབས་ཀྱིས་བཅད། །ཀློང་ཆེན་གཅིག་ལ་རྟོགས་དང་མ་རྟོགས་དང་། །གྲོལ་དང་མ་གྲོལ་གཉིས་མེད་མཉམ་པ་ཆེ།

Therefore, it is in the naturally occurring state without transition
or change
that the most majestic perfection of goals is experienced as
nonduality.
The total freedom of the three realms—the ultimate meaning
of the nonduality of samsara and nirvana—
is the fortress of dharmakaya, the nature of being that arises
inherently from within,
such that it is completely pure like space, yet is in fact beyond
all metaphors.

As long as you remain fixated on individual things, on "this"
or "that,"
you remain caught in dualism—the cage of confusion entailing
self and other.
When you make no biased distinction—of "this"—
everything is the same in the state of equalness, with no frame
of reference,
and so Vajrasattva declares, "Nonduality is realized!"

This is the eighth section of *The Precious Treasury of the Basic Space of Phenomena,* demonstrating nonduality within awakened mind.

❖

WITHIN THE SINGLE EXPANSE, supremely spacious by nature,
awakened mind, equal to space, is pivotal.
Focus on this key point and distill it to its vital essence;
it is the greatest of the great—wholly positive and spacious
enlightened mind.
In its very essence, it thoroughly shatters the outer confines
of reality.
Within this single vast expanse, there is no duality of realization
versus its lack,
of freedom versus its lack, but a supreme state of equalness.

།སྒོ་ངའི་ནང་ནས་འདབ་གཤོག་རྒྱས་པའི་བྱ། །རྒྱ་དང་བྲལ་བས་ནམ་མཁའི་ཀློང་ན་གནས། །ཀླུ་རྣམས་ཟིལ་གནོན་གཡང་ས་ཤུགས་ཀྱིས་ཆོད། །ཐེག་པའི་ཡང་རྩེ་རྡོ་རྗེ་སྙིང་པོ་ཡང་། །ཇི་བཞིན་རྟོགས་པའི་རྣལ་འབྱོར་སྐལ་པ་ཅན། །ཐེག་དམན་ཟིལ་གནོན་འཁོར་བའི་གཡང་ས་ཆོད།

།ཀུན་གྲོལ་མཉམ་པ་ཆེན་པོར་གནས་པ་དེ། །རྒྱུ་འབྲས་རྩོལ་སྒྲུབ་ཅན་ལ་མི་རིགས་ཀྱང་། །ཐེག་མཆོག་མི་གཡོ་མཉམ་པའི་དོན་ལ་འཐད།

།ཐམས་ཅད་བདེ་ཆེན་མཁའ་མཉམ་ཆོས་སྐུའི་ཀློང་། །ཆོས་སྐུའི་ཀློང་དུ་མ་གྲོལ་འགའ་ཡང་མེད། །ཆོས་ཉིད་དང་བཞེངས་རྡོ་རྗེ་སྙིང་པོའི་སྐུ།། བག་ཆགས་ལུས་ལ་སྙིང་པོའི་རྩལ་རྫོགས་ཏེ། །སྐྱེ་ཤི་བར་དོ་སྲིད་པའི་ལུས་པོར་ནས། །རིག་པ་གཅིག་པུ་ཀུན་དང་དབྱེར་མེད་ཅིང་། །ལྷུན་གྲུབ་ས་ལ་རྒྱལ་པོའི་སྲིད་ཟིན་ནས། །རྒྱ་ཆད་མེད་པར་སྤྲུལ་པ་འབྱུང་བ་དང་། །ཐོགས་པ་མེད་པར་ཀུན་ལ་འཇུག་པ་ནི། །བྱེར་མེད་ལྷུང་ཞེན་རྣལ་འབྱོར་སྤྱོད་ཡུལ་ཏེ། །དམན་པའི་ཐེག་པ་ཀུན་ལ་མི་རིགས་ཀྱང་། །ཨ་ཏིས་རིགས་པར་སྟོན་པ་འབྲས་བུའི་གནད།

A garuda whose wings have grown within the egg
abides in the expanse of the sky once it breaks out of the egg.
It overwhelms nagas and crosses directly over abysses.
So also, a fortunate yogin who has realized the vajra heart
essence, just as it is,
the pinnacle of all spiritual approaches,
outshines those following lower approaches and crosses directly
over the abyss of samsara.

The freedom of everything—abiding in a supreme state of
equalness—
is unacceptable to those involved in cause and effect, effort and
achievement,
but in the most sublime approach it makes perfect sense as the
ultimate meaning of unwavering equalness.

Everything is supreme bliss, equal to space itself—the expanse of
dharmakaya.
There is nothing that is not free within the expanse of
dharmakaya.
The true nature of everything is experienced intuitively as the
kaya of the vajra heart essence.
The dynamic energy of this heart essence is perfect within the
body born of habitual patterns.
Once the body of conditioned existence between birth and death
is cast off,
awareness is experienced as a oneness, in no way divisible.
Once one has "gained the empire" on the level of spontaneous
presence,
emanations occur without restriction
and one can engage in every situation without impediment.
Such is the domain of a yogin who "is effortlessly borne on
the wind."
While this is unacceptable to anyone involved in lower spiritual
approaches,
it is shown by the ati approach to make perfect sense—it is the
key point of the fruition.

།སྐྱེ་མེད་སྐྱེ་བའི་ཆོ་འཕྲུལ་འབྱུང་བ་ལ། །རྒྱུ་འབྲས་མཚན་མར་འཛིན་པ་འཁྲུལ་པའི་བློ། །ཨ་དེས་རྒྱུ་རྐྱེན་མེད་པར་བསྟན་པ་ནི། །འོག་མ་རྣམས་ལ་མི་རིགས་རིགས་པའི་གནད།

།སངས་རྒྱས་སེམས་ཅན་དགོངས་སྤྱོད་དབྱེར་མེད་ལ། །འཁོར་འདས་གཉིས་སུ་འཛིན་པ་འཁྲུལ་པའི་བློ། །ཨ་དེས་གཉིས་སུ་མེད་པར་བསྟན་པ་ནིས། །འོག་མ་རྣམས་ལ་མི་རིགས་རིགས་པའི་གནད།

།རྟོགས་དང་མ་རྟོགས་མེད་པར་གྲོལ་བ་ལ། །རྟོགས་ནས་གྲོལ་བར་འདོད་པ་མཉམ་པའི་དགྲ། །ཨ་དེས་མཉམ་ཉིད་གཅིག་ཏུ་བསྟན་པ་དེ།། འོག་མ་རྣམས་ལ་མི་རིགས་རིགས་པའི་གནད།

།མཚོན་བྱེད་ཐབས་ཀྱི་ཁྱད་པར་མ་བསྐྱེན་པར། །བརྗོད་མེད་རྟོགས་པར་མི་འདོད་བླུན་པོའི་བློ། །ཨ་དེས་དོན་དང་དབྱེར་མེད་བསྟན་པ་དེ། ། འོག་མ་རྣམས་ལ་མི་རིགས་རིགས་པའི་གནད།

།རྫོགས་ཆེན་ཡེ་གདལ་གཏིང་མཐའ་མེད་པ་ལ། །ཐུག་པ་མེད་ཅེས་ཟེར་བ་བླུན་པོའི་བློ། །ཨ་དེས་མུ་མེད་ཚིག་ཚོད་བསྟན་པ་དེ། །

Since the magical illusion of origination occurs within what has no origin,
it is the ordinary confused mind that characterizes things as involving causality.
What the ati approach reveals as the absence of causes or conditions
makes eminently perfect sense, although it is unacceptable in lower approaches.

The intent and conduct of buddhas and ordinary beings are not separate,
so it is the ordinary confused mind that holds samsara and nirvana to be a duality.
What the ati approach reveals as nondual
makes eminently perfect sense, although it is unacceptable in lower approaches.

Given the freedom in which it is irrelevant whether or not one has realization,
to believe that freedom comes about through realization is the enemy of equalness.
What the ati approach reveals as a single state of equalness
makes eminently perfect sense, although it is unacceptable in lower approaches.

To hold that one cannot realize the inexpressible
without relying on specific means to characterize it is a fool's attitude.
What the ati approach reveals as inseparability from the ultimate
makes eminently perfect sense, although it is unacceptable in lower approaches.

Although great perfection is timeless and infinite, without fixed depth or extent,
to claim that it is "unfathomable" is a fool's attitude.
What the ati approach reveals as a boundless, unique state

འོག་མའི་སློ་ཡུལ་མི་རིགས་རིགས་པའི་གནད།

།ཐིག་ལེ་གཅིག་ལ་རྒྱ་མཚན་གོ་བཟློག་པས། །འབྲས་བུ་རེ་དོགས་ཚོད་དེ་མཁའ་དང་མཉམ། །ཡངས་སོ་ཆེའོ་མཁའ་མཉམ་རྒྱལ་བའི་ཐུགས། ། སྤྱངས་ཐོབ་མེད་དེ་ཐིག་ལེ་གཅིག་གི་ཀློང་། །ཡེ་ནས་གྲོལ་ལོ་རྟོགས་དང་མ་རྟོགས་མེད། །རྣལ་འབྱོར་མཁའ་མཉམ་བྱ་བྲལ་ལམ་དུ་བདེ།

།ཡེ་སངས་རྒྱས་པའི་རིག་པ་ཡུལ་མེད་འདི། །འཁོར་བར་མི་འཁྲུམ་འཁྲུལ་གཞི་ཀུན་ལས་འདས། །སུ་ཡང་མ་འཁྲུལ་འཁྲུལ་པའི་གནས་མེད་དེ། །ཐམས་ཅད་ཆོས་དབྱིངས་ཀློང་གསལ་གཅིག་གི་ངང་། ། སྤྲོ་ཕྱི་རིས་མེད་མཁའ་མཉམ་ཡངས་པ་ཉིད། །ཡེ་བབས་ལྷུན་གྲུབ་འཁོར་བ་གདོད་ནས་དག

།གྲོལ་བར་མི་འཇུག་སྙུ་ངན་འདས་མི་ལེན། །མི་འགྱུར་ཀློང་ཆེན་འཁོར་འདས་ཡོད་མ་མྱོང་། །འདི་ལ་སྤྱངས་ཐོབ་རེ་དོགས་མི་དམིགས་ཤིང་།། གདོད་ནས་བྱང་ཆུབ་གཞི་ཀློང་ཡངས་པ་ཆེ། །ཐམས་ཅད་མིང་ཙམ་དོན་ལ་མཆོན་བརྗོད་འདས། །

makes eminently perfect sense, although it is unacceptable in
lower approaches.

The usual order of things is reversed within the single sphere
of being,
and so hope and fear concerning the fruition are cut through—
a state equal to space.
So vast, so supreme, the enlightened mind of victorious ones is
equal to space.
There is no renunciation or attainment—the expanse of the
single sphere.
This is timeless freedom; it is irrelevant whether or not one has
realization.
A yogin is content on the path equal to space, with nothing
needing to be done.

This timelessly awakened awareness that entails no object
does not wander in samsara, for it is beyond all basis for
confusion.
No one at all is confused, for there is no context for confusion.
Everything lies within the scope of the basic space of
phenomena, a single lucid expanse.
With no time frame, this spaciousness is equal to space itself.
Samsara is primordially pure, a timeless and spontaneously
present state of utter relaxation.

One does not enter a state of freedom or attain nirvana.
The unchanging vast expanse—samsara and nirvana have never
known existence.
Here there is no frame of reference for renunciation or
attainment, hope or fear,
but rather a supremely spacious expanse that is the primordially
enlightened ground of being.
All things are mere labels, for in actuality they are beyond
characterization or expression.

གྲོལ་དང་འབྲལ་མེད་འཁོར་འདས་ལ་བློས་པས། །སུ་ཡང་མ་རྩོལ་བཅོས་བསྒྱུར་མ་བྱེད་ཅིག

།ཡངས་དོག་མཐོ་དམན་མེད་པའི་རིག་པ་ལ། །རྒྱ་ཆད་ཕྱོགས་ལྷུང་མེད་ཀྱིས་དམིགས་གཏད་ཞོལ། །བྱ་བྱེད་འགྲོ་འོང་མེད་པའི་རིག་པ་ལ། །དུས་དང་གཉེན་པོ་མེད་ཀྱིས་འཛིན་རྩོལ་ཞོག །ཆེད་དུ་དམིགས་པ་ཡོད་ན་འཆིང་བའི་རྒྱུ། །གང་ལའང་གཏད་འཛིན་མ་འཆའ་ཕྲུམ་ལ་ཐོང་།

།ཆོས་ཀུན་ཡེ་ནས་གྲོལ་རུང་མ་གྲོལ་རུང་། །གནས་ལུགས་རང་བཞིན་དག་རུང་མ་དག་རུང་། །སེམས་ཉིད་སྤྲོས་དང་བྲལ་རུང་མ་བྲལ་རུང་།། གཉུག་མའི་གཤིས་ལ་གྲུབ་རུང་མ་གྲུབ་རུང་།

།འཁོར་འདས་རང་བཞིན་གཉིས་རུང་མི་གཉིས་རུང་། །བསམ་བརྗོད་ཀུན་ལས་འདས་རུང་མ་འདས་རུང་། །དགག་སྒྲུབ་འབྲལ་པ་ཞིག་རུང་མ་ཞིག་རུང་། །རྟོགས་པའི་ལྟ་བ་རྟོགས་རུང་མ་རྟོགས་རུང་།

།ཆོས་ཉིད་དོན་ལ་བསྒོམས་རུང་མ་བསྒོམས་རུང་། །བླང་དོར་མེད་པས་དཔྱད་རུང་མ་དཔྱད་རུང་། །

Having decisively experienced that samsara is not confusion
and nirvana is not freedom,
let no one make any effort!
Let no one try to meddle with or alter this!

Awareness, with no breadth or depth,
is not subject to restrictions or extremes, so give up any frame
of reference.
Awareness, involving no plans or actions, no coming or going,
entails no time frame or antidote, so drop reification and effort.
If there is a deliberate frame of reference, it is a cause of bondage.
Do not rely on any fixed construct whatsoever—let go in
evenness!

It is of no concern whether or not all phenomena are
timelessly free.
It is of no concern whether or not the way of abiding is pure
by nature.
It is of no concern whether or not mind itself is free of
elaboration.
It is of no concern whether or not anything has ever existed
within the fundamentally unconditioned, genuine state.

It is of no concern whether or not samsara and nirvana are
by nature a duality.
It is of no concern whether or not all thoughts and expressions
are transcended.
It is of no concern whether or not confused attempts at proof
and refutation are demolished.
It is of no concern whether or not the view to be realized has
been realized.

It is of no concern whether or not you meditate on the ultimate
meaning of the true nature of phenomena.
It is of no concern whether or not you engage in examination,
since there is nothing to accept or reject.

གནས་ལུགས་འབྲས་བུ་གྲུབ་རུང་མ་གྲུབ་རུང་། །ས་དང་ལམ་རྣམས་བགྲོད་རུང་མ་བགྲོད་རུང་།

།སྒྲིབ་པ་ཀུན་དང་བྲལ་རུང་མ་བྲལ་རུང་། །བསྐྱེད་རྫོགས་ཆོས་ཉིད་རྫོགས་རུང་མ་རྫོགས་རུང་། །ཐར་པའི་འབྲས་བུ་ཐོབ་རུང་མ་ཐོ་རུང་། །འགྲོ་དྲུག་འཁོར་བར་འཁྱམས་རུང་མ་འཁྱམས་རུང་།

།རང་བཞིན་ལྷུན་གྱིས་གྲུབ་རུང་མ་གྲུབ་རུང་། །ཧག་ཆད་གཉིས་འཛིན་བཅིངས་རུང་མ་བཅིངས་རུང་། །ཆོས་ཉིད་དགོངས་པར་སླེབ་རུང་མ་སླེབ་རུང་། །གོང་མའི་རྗེས་སུ་སློགས་རུང་མ་སློགས་རུང་།

།གནམ་ས་འདྲེ་ལྡོག་སྣང་བ་ཅི་ཤར་ཡང་། །ཕྱལ་བ་ལྷུག་པ་གཞི་མེད་ཟང་ཀ་མ། །གཏད་མེད་ཟང་ཟིང་བན་བུན་ཆལ་མ་ཆོལ། །རི་དྭགས་གཉིས་མེད་སྨྱོན་པའི་ངང་ཚུལ་ཅན། །ལྷ་སྒོམ་རིས་མེད་ཆེད་འཛིན་འདོད་བློ་ཞིག །ཞི་འདོད་འཁྲིས་མེད་འདི་ཞེས་རྩོལ་སྒྲུབ་མེད།

།གང་བྱུང་བྱུང་ལ་གང་སྣང་སྣང་དུ་ཆུག །གང་ཤར་ཤར་ལ་གང་ཡིན་ཡིན་དུ་ཆུག །གང་ཡང་ཡིན་ལ་གང་ཡང་མིན་དུ་ཆུག

It is of no concern whether or not the way of abiding has ever
existed as the fruition.
It is of no concern whether or not you have traversed the paths
and levels of realization.

It is of no concern whether or not you are free of all
obscurations.
It is of no concern whether or not the development and
completion stages perfect your true nature.
It is of no concern whether or not the fruition of liberation
is attained.
It is of no concern whether or not you wander in the six states
of samsara.

It is of no concern whether or not the nature of being is
spontaneous presence.
It is of no concern whether or not you are bound by dualistic
perceptions of affirmation and denial.
It is of no concern whether or not you have arrived at the
enlightened intent of the true nature of phenomena.
It is of no concern whether or not you follow in the footsteps of
masters of the past.

No matter what arises, even if heaven and earth change places,
there is a bare state of relaxed openness, without any underlying
basis.
Without any reference point—nebulous, ephemeral, and
evanescent—
this is the mode of a lunatic, free of the duality of hope and fear.
With unbiased view and meditation, ordinary consciousness that
is caught up in reification collapses.
Without the entanglements of wishful thinking, there is no
"thing" to strive for or achieve.

Let whatever happens happen and whatever manifests manifest.
Let whatever occurs occur and whatever is be.
Let whatever is anything at all be nothing at all.

།ཀུན་སྤྱོད་ངེས་མེད་རིག་པ་སྤྲོད་རྒྱལ་དང་། །ཆོས་དང་ཆོས་མིན་རྩིས་གཞི་འགག་མེད་པས། །གཏད་མེད་ཟང་ཀ་གྲུབ་མཐའི་གཟེབ་ལས་འདས། །ཟ་འཆག་ཉལ་འདུག་ཉིན་ཞག་ཕྱམ་གདལ་བས། །རང་བཞིན་ཆོས་ཉིད་མཉམ་པའི་ངང་ཉིད་དེ། །མཆོད་པའི་ལྷ་མེད་བརྟུང་བའི་འདྲེ་ཡང་མེད། །སྒོམ་པའི་ཆོས་མེད་ཐ་མལ་རང་དགའི་ངང་། །མ་བཅོས་རྒྱལ་པོ་སྙེམས་མེད་ཕྱམ་གཅིག་པས། །ཕྱལ་བ་ལྷུག་པ་ཡན་པ་གཅིག་པུ་ཉིད། །མ་བྱས་ཡེ་ཟིན་རྩོལ་སྒྲུབ་བྲལ་བས་བདེ།

།ལྟ་བའི་གཞི་མེད་སྒོམ་པའི་ངང་མེད་ལ། །སྤྱོད་པའི་ཆོས་མེད་བསྒྲུབ་བྱའི་འབྲས་བུ་མེད། །ཐམས་ཅད་རིས་མེད་མཉམ་པར་ཕྱམ་གདལ་བས།། བྱ་རྩོལ་མ་དགོས་ཡངས་དོག་མེད་པར་བདེ།

།སྟོན་པ་མེད་པས་སྒྲུབ་བློའི་ཆོས་ཟད་དེ། །སྤང་བྱ་མེད་པས་གཉེན་པོའི་འཆིང་ཞེན་འདས། །གང་ཡིན་ཀུན་ཡིན་ཡིན་མིན་འགག་མེད་པས། །གང་སྣང་གང་ཤར་འདེམ་ཀ་མེད་པར་གྲོལ།

With your conduct unpredictable, you make the final leap
into awareness
without the slightest basis for determining what is spiritual
or not,
and so this bare state with no reference point is beyond the cage
of philosophy.
Whether eating, moving around, lying down, or sitting, day and
night you rest in infinite evenness,
so that you experience the true nature of phenomena as their
equalness.
There are no gods to worship, no demons to exorcise,
nothing to cultivate in meditation—this is the completely
"ordinary" state.
With this single state of evenness—the uncontrived ruler that
has no pride—
there is oneness, a relaxed and unstructured openness.
How delightful—things are timelessly ensured without having
to be done,
and being free of effort and achievement, you are content.

Given that there is no basis for the view or specific context for
meditation,
there is no factor of conduct or fruition to accomplish.
Since everything is infinitely uniform in undifferentiated
equalness, there is no need for concerted effort.
In the absence of any fixed dimension, you are content.

Since there is no speculation, ordinary ideas of achievement
come to an end.
Since there is nothing to abandon, antidotes—constricting
fixations—are transcended.
There is not the slightest sense of there being anything, or
everything, or even something that "is" or "is not,"
and so whatever manifests, whatever arises, is inevitably free.

།མ་གྲོལ་ཡེ་གྲོལ་རང་གྲོལ་ཆོས་མེད་པས། །ཕྱམ་གཅིག་གཏད་མེད་ལ་བབླའི་ཆོས་ལས་འདས།

།སློང་ཡངས་སློང་ཡངས་སློང་ཆེན་ཡངས་པའི་ངང་། །སློང་ཆེན་རབ་འབྱམས་སློང་གསལ་སློང་འབྱམས་པས། །སློང་གཅིག་གཉིས་མེད་བདེ་སློང་འཁྲིལ་བ་ནི། །སྣ་ཚོགས་རང་གྲོལ་ཆོས་ཉིད་ཟད་སར་ཕྱིན། །མི་འགྱུར་ལྷུན་གྲུབ་འདུན་མ་ལེགས་པའི་རྩེ།

།བདག་བཞིན་རྗེས་སུ་འཇུག་པའི་འགྲོ་རྣམས་ཀྱང་། །འདི་བཞིན་ཡེ་འབྱམས་སློང་ཆེན་གཅིག་ཏུ་དྲིལ། །ཀུན་བཟང་ས་ལ་གདན་སྲིད་ཟིན་པ་ཡིན།

།ཆོས་དབྱིངས་རིན་པོ་ཆེའི་མཛོད་ལས། །ཆོས་ཐམས་ཅད་བྱང་ཆུབ་སེམས་ཀྱི་སློང་དུ་ལ་བབླ་བར་བསྟན་པའི་ལེའུ་སྟེ་དགུ་པའོ།།

།།རང་བཞིན་གདོད་ནས་དག་པའི་བྱང་ཆུབ་སེམས། །བཏང་གཞག་འགྲོ་འོང་མེད་པའི་ཆོས་ཉིད་ལ། །བཙལ་བས་མི་འགྲུབ་ཆོས་ཉིད་ནམ་མཁའི་སློང་། །རང་བཞིན་བཞག་པས་འོད་གསལ་ཉི་ཟླ་འཆར།

Phenomena are ineffable—they do not exist as timelessly free,
naturally free, or not free—
and so the single state of evenness with no reference point
is beyond being any phenomenon that could be decisively
experienced.

Within the spacious expanse, the spacious expanse, the spacious
vast expanse,
I, Longchen Rabjam, for whom the lucid expanse of being is
infinite,
experience everything as embraced within a blissful expanse,
a single nondual expanse.
I, Natsok Rangdrol, have reached the point of natural freedom
where phenomena resolve.
Unchanging spontaneous presence is the pinnacle of my
excellent counsel.

Moreover, you who follow my example—
bring everything together thus within the timeless range of
a single vast expanse.
In this way, you will gain the ongoing state of authentic being
on the level of Samantabhadra.

This is the ninth section of *The Precious Treasury of the Basic Space of Phenomena,* demonstrating the decisive experience that one comes to concerning all phenomena within the expanse of awakened mind.

❖

AWAKENED MIND is by nature primordially pure.
The true nature of phenomena is such that there is nothing to
discard or adopt,
nothing that comes or goes, nothing to achieve by trying.
Rather, the sun and moon of utter lucidity arise
when one rests naturally in the spacious expanse that is the true
nature of phenomena.

།ཡུལ་ཀྱང་མི་དགག་སེམས་ཀྱང་མི་གཟུང་བར། །རང་བཞིན་ལྷུན་མཉམ་ངང་ལས་མི་གཡོ་ན། །ཀུན་བཟང་ཡངས་པ་ཆེན་པོའི་དགོངས་པར་ཕྱིན།

།མི་སྤྲོ་མི་བསྡུ་རང་དངས་སང་ངེ་བ། །དངས་པའི་རྒྱ་མཚོ་མི་གཡོ་མཉམ་པ་བཞིན། །ཆོས་ཉིད་གདིང་གསལ་རང་བྱུང་ཡེ་ཤེས་དང་། །འབྱུང་འཇུག་རེ་དོགས་བྲལ་བར་གནས་པ་ཡིན།

།ཆིག་གིས་མི་མཚོན་འཇུར་བུའི་སེམས་མེད་པར། །རང་བབས་གྱིན་འདའ་བཅོས་བསླད་མེད་པ་ནི། །ཀློང་ཐིམ་ཆོས་ཉིད་མཚན་མ་མེད་པ་སྟེ།། སྒོམ་དང་བསྒོམ་པར་བྱ་བའི་ཆོས་མེད་པས། །བྱིང་རྒོད་རང་ཡན་རང་བྱུང་དགོངས་པར་ཞར།

།སྤྱངས་པས་མི་སྤོང་ཀུན་རྟོག་རིག་པའི་རྩལ། །ཆོས་ཉིད་དང་དུ་དབྱེ་བསལ་རིས་མེད་པས། །བསྒྲུབས་པས་མི་འགྲུབ་ཆོས་ཉིད་དབྱིངས་སུ་ཞར། །འཁོར་བ་མ་སྤྱངས་རང་བྱུང་ཡེ་ཤེས་སུ། །ཀློང་ཆེན་རྩལ་གྱི་རྣལ་འབྱོར་དག་པས་མཐོང་།

།ཡེ་ནས་སྣང་སེམས་རང་བབས་ཆོས་ཉིད་དང་། །

Without sense objects being blocked or mind being reified,
if there is no straying from the natural state of spontaneous equalness
you arrive at the enlightened intent of supreme spaciousness, Samantabhadra.

Without the arising and subsiding of thoughts, there is a naturally limpid, pristine state,
like the unwavering evenness of a limpid ocean.
Free of the occurrence of or involvement in thoughts, free of hope or fear,
you abide within the state of naturally occurring timeless awareness, the true nature of which is profoundly lucid.

Without the compulsions of ordinary mind,
there is an unfeigned state—a natural settling, uncontrived and unadulterated—
though it cannot be characterized with words.
This absorption in the expanse of being, the true nature of which cannot be characterized,
involves neither meditation nor something to meditate on,
and so laxity and agitation dissipate naturally, and enlightened intent occurs naturally.

All-consuming thought patterns cannot be abandoned by being renounced, for they are the dynamic energy of awareness.
Their true nature is such that there are no distinctions, nothing to differentiate or exclude,
so that nature is not ensured by achievement, but arises as basic space.
Without rejecting samsara, you perceive it to be naturally occurring timeless awareness
through the pure yoga of the dynamic energy of the vast expanse of being.

In the timeless unity of sensory appearances and mind—
the naturally settled state that is the true nature of phenomena—

ཏིང་འཛིན་མི་གཡོ་ཆུ་བོའི་རྒྱུན་ཤར་བས། །རྡོ་རྗེ་རྩེ་མོ་ཀུན་བཟང་ཐུགས་ཀྱི་མཆོག །ཡངས་པའི་ཆོས་མཆོག་ནམ་མཁའི་མཐའ་དང་མཉམ། །དབྱེ་བསལ་མེད་པར་ཐམས་ཅད་སྒོམ་པའི་མཆོག །ཡེ་འབྱམས་རྨད་བྱུང་རྒྱལ་པོར་ལྷུན་གྱིས་གྲུབ།

།ཡེ་ནས་སྤྱི་བླུགས་འོད་གསལ་ཆུ་བོའི་རྒྱུན། །བཏང་གཞག་མེད་པའི་ངང་འདིར་ལྷུན་གྲུབ་པས། །འཁོར་འདས་རང་བཞིན་ཆོས་དབྱིངས་དགོངས་པའི་མཆོག །མི་གཡོ་བརྗོད་འདས་མཁའ་མཉམ་ཀློང་ཆེན་ཉིད།། འགྲོ་བ་ཀུན་ལ་ཡེ་ནས་བབས་ཀྱིས་གྲུབ།

།བདག་ལས་གཞན་དུ་སྣང་བ་འཁྲུལ་པའི་སེམས། །བསྒོམ་དང་རྩོལ་བར་འདོད་པ་འཁྲུལ་པའི་སེམས། །འཁྲུལ་པ་ཆོས་ཉིད་དང་བཞག་མཉམ་པའི་ཞིང་། །མི་གཡོ་གདོད་ནས་དག་པའི་རང་བཞིན་ཀློང་། །བྱ་དང་རྩོལ་མེད་གཞག་དང་མ་བཞག་མེད།

།མི་འགྱུར་ལྷུན་གྱིས་གྲུབ་པའི་ཆོས་ཉིད་ལ། །དམིགས་བསམ་ཆོལ་ཁྲོ་བྲལ་བའི་རང་རིག་གིས། །ཡང་ཡང་བལྟས་ན་བལྟ་རྒྱུ་མེད་པ་མཐོང་། །བལྟར་མེད་རིག་པ་སྤྱི་བླུགས་ལྟ་བ་ཡིན།

meditative absorption is experienced as an unwavering,
ongoing flow.
Thus, the vajra pinnacle, the most excellent enlightened mind
of Samantabhadra,
is the most sublime, spacious state, equal to space.
The most sublime meditation of all involves no differentiation
or exclusion.
It is spontaneously present as the superb, timelessly infinite
monarch.

The ongoing flow of utter lucidity, timeless and omnipresent,
is spontaneously present within this context, in which nothing is
discarded or adopted,
and so it is the most sublime enlightened intent—the basic space
of phenomena, the nature of samsara and nirvana.
This vast expanse, unwavering, indescribable, and equal
to space,
is timelessly and innately present in all beings.

It is the ordinary confused mind that perceives
sensory appearances to be something other than oneself.
It is the ordinary confused mind that believes in meditation and
making an effort.
The true nature of confusion is the realm of equalness, the
natural state of rest—
the natural expanse that is unwavering and primordially pure.
There is nothing to do and no effort to make—whether or not
you are resting is irrelevant.

Given the unchanging, spontaneously present nature of
phenomena,
if you look again and again with self-knowing awareness, free of
any complicating conceptual framework,
you will see that there is nothing to look at.
Nothing to look at—this is the view of omnipresent awareness.

།མ་བསྒོམས་རིག་པ་བདུད་གཞག་བྲལ་བ་ལ། །ཡང་ཡང་བསྒོམས་ན་བསྒོམ་དུ་མེད་པ་མཐོང་། །སྒོམ་མེད་རིག་པ་སྤྱི་བླུགས་སྒོམ་པ་ཡིན།

།གཉིས་མེད་སྣང་དོར་བྲལ་བའི་གནས་ལུགས་ལ། །ཡང་ཡང་སྤྱད་ན་སྤྱད་དུ་མེད་པ་མཐོང་། །སྤྱད་མེད་རིག་པ་སྤྱི་བླུགས་སྤྱོད་པ་ཡིན།

།ཡེ་ཐྲིན་རེ་དོགས་བྲལ་བའི་ལྷུན་གྲུབ་ལ། །ཡང་ཡང་བསྒྲུབས་ན་བསྒྲུབ་དུ་མེད་པ་མཐོང་། །བསྒྲུབ་མེད་རིག་པ་སྤྱི་བླུགས་འབྲས་བུ་ཡིན།

།མཉམ་ཉིད་ངང་ལས་ཡུལ་དུ་མི་རྟོག་ཅིང་། །སེམས་སུ་མི་འཛིན་རེ་དོགས་འབྱུང་འཇུག་ཞི། །ཡུལ་སེམས་མཉམ་པའི་ངང་དེར་གནས་པ་ནི།། ཆོས་ཉིད་ཀློང་ལས་ངང་གིས་གཡོས་པ་མེད། །མཚན་མའི་ཡུལ་ལ་ཡུལ་མེད་སྤྱི་བླུགས་གནས། །ཡེ་ནས་གཉིས་མེད་རིག་པ་སྤྱི་བླུགས་པས། །འཁོར་འདས་དབྱེར་མེད་རྫོགས་པ་ཆེན་པོའི་ངང་། །ཐམས་ཅད་སྣང་དོར་མེད་པར་ཕྱམ་གདལ་ལོ།

Given awareness, which is not cultivated in meditation and in which nothing is discarded or adopted,
if you meditate again and again, you will see that there is nothing to cultivate in meditation.
Nothing to cultivate in meditation—this is the meditation of omnipresent awareness.

Given the way of abiding, nondual and free of acceptance and rejection,
if you engage in conduct again and again,
you will see that there is no conduct to enact.
No conduct to enact—this is the conduct of omnipresent awareness.

Given spontaneous presence, timelessly ensured and free of hope and fear,
if you strive to achieve again and again,
you will see that there is nothing to achieve.
Nothing to achieve—this is the fruition of omnipresent awareness.

Within the state of equalness, there are no thoughts about sense objects and no reification of ordinary mind,
so the occurrence of and involvement in hope and fear are pacified.
Abiding in the equalness of sense objects and mind
means that, as a matter of course, there is no straying from the expanse that is the true nature of phenomena.
One abides in an omnipresent state in which what are characterized as sense objects do not exist as objects.
Since there is omnipresent awareness, timeless and nondual,
within the state of great perfection—the indivisibility of samsara and nirvana—
everything is in a state of infinite evenness, without acceptance or rejection.

།དངོས་དང་དངོས་མེད་དབྱིངས་སུ་མཉམ་པ་དང་། །སངས་རྒྱས་སེམས་ཅན་དབྱིངས་སུ་མཉམ་པ་དང་། །ཀུན་རྫོབ་དོན་དམ་དབྱིངས་སུ་མཉམ་པ་དང་། །སྐྱོན་དང་ཡོན་ཏན་དབྱིངས་སུ་མཉམ་པ་དང་། །མཐོ་དམན་ཕྱོགས་མཚམས་དབྱིངས་སུ་མཉམ་པའི་ཕྱིར། །རང་བྱུང་ངང་ལས་རོལ་པ་ཅི་ཤར་ཡང་། །ཤར་བའི་དུས་ན་མཉམ་ཤར་བཟང་ངན་མེད། །དེ་ལ་བླང་དོར་གཉེན་པོས་བཅོས་ཅི་དགོས། །གནས་པའི་ཚེ་ན་མཉམ་གནས་བཟང་ངན་མེད། །ད་ལྟ་སེམས་ལས་གང་བྱུང་རང་ཞིར་ཞོག །གྲོལ་བའི་ཚེ་ན་མཉམ་གྲོལ་བཟང་ངན་མེད། །དྲན་པའི་རྗེས་ལ་དགག་སྒྲུབ་འཕྲོ་མ་མཐུད།

།ཐམས་ཅད་གཞི་ཀློང་བྱང་ཆུབ་སེམས་ཉིད་ལས། །རྩལ་དང་རོལ་པའི་འཆར་ཚུལ་མ་ངེས་པས། །མཉམ་པར་ཤར་ཡང་གདོད་མའི་ཀློང་ནས་ཤར། །མི་མཉམ་ཤར་ཡང་མཉམ་པའི་དབྱིངས་ནས་ཤར། །མཉམ་པར་གནས་ཀྱང་རང་གཞག་ཆོས་ཉིད་དང་། །མི་མཉམ་གནས་ཀྱང་མཉམ་པའི་དབྱིངས་ན་གནས། །མཉམ་པར་གྲོལ་ཡང་རང་བྱུང་ཡེ་ཤེས་ཀློང་།། མི་མཉམ་གྲོལ་ཡང་མཉམ་པའི་དབྱིངས་སུ་གྲོལ།

What is tangible and what is intangible are equal in basic space,
buddhas and ordinary beings are equal in basic space,
relative reality and ultimate reality are equal in basic space,
flaws and positive qualities are equal in basic space,
and all directions—above, below, and in between—are equal in basic space.
Therefore, whatever display arises from that naturally occurring state,
even as it arises, things arise equally, none being better or worse.
What need is there to accept or reject them by applying antidotes?
When things abide, they abide equally, none being better or worse.
Whatever is now taking place in your mind, rest in natural peace.
When things are free, they are equally free, none being better or worse.
In the wake of being conscious of them, do not continue to suppress or indulge in them.

Within awakened mind itself—the expanse of the ground of being—
the way in which everything arises as its dynamic energy and display is unpredictable.
Even as things arise equally, they arise within that primordial expanse.
Even as they arise unequally, they arise within the basic space of their equalness.
Even as they abide equally, their true nature is a natural state of rest.
Even as they abide unequally, they abide within the basic space of their equalness.
Even as they are freed equally, this constitutes the expanse of naturally occurring timeless awareness.
Even as they are freed unequally, they are freed within the basic space of their equalness.

།ཐམས་ཅད་ཡེ་མཉམ་རང་བྱུང་རིག་པ་ལ། །ཤར་དང་མ་ཤར་དབྱིངས་ལ་ཡེ་ནས་མེད། །གནས་དང་མི་གནས་དབྱིངས་ལ་ཡེ་ནས་མེད། །གྲོལ་དང་མ་གྲོལ་དབྱིངས་ལ་ཡེ་ནས་མེད།

།མི་གཡོ་མཉམ་པ་ཆེན་པོའི་རིག་པ་ལ། །ཤར་བའི་དུས་ན་རང་ཤར་རང་ས་ཟིན། །གནས་པའི་དུས་ན་རང་གནས་རང་ས་ཟིན། །གྲོལ་བའི་དུས་ན་རང་གྲོལ་རང་ས་ཟིན།

།མི་འགྱུར་སྤྲོས་དང་བྲལ་བའི་རིག་པ་ལ། །ཤར་བ་ཡི་ཤར་གནས་པ་ཡི་གནས་ལ། །གྲོལ་བ་ཡི་གྲོལ་ནམ་མཁའི་རང་བཞིན་ནོ།

།ཤར་གནས་གྲོལ་གསུམ་ཤར་གྲོལ་རྒྱུན་ཆད་མེད། །རྒྱུན་ཆད་མེད་པས་རྒྱུ་འབྲས་བར་མ་ཆོད། །རྒྱུ་འབྲས་མེད་པས་འཁོར་བའི་གཡང་ས་ཆོད། །གཡང་ས་མེད་པས་གོལ་ས་ག་ལ་ཡོད།

།ཡེ་ནས་མི་འགྱུར་ཀུན་ཏུ་བཟང་པོའི་ཀློང་། །འཕོ་འགྱུར་མེད་པ་རྡོ་རྗེ་སེམས་དཔའི་ཀློང་། །གནས་ལུགས་རང་ངོ་ཤེས་པ་ཙམ་ཉིད་ལ། །སངས་རྒྱས་ཞེས་སུ་མིང་འདི་བཏགས་པར་ཟད།

།འདི་ཉིད་རྟོགས་ནས་སྣང་དོར་ཆོས་མེད་པས། །

Given naturally occurring awareness, the timeless equalness
of everything,
arising and nonarising are timelessly nonexistent in basic space,
abiding and nonabiding are timelessly nonexistent in basic
space,
and freedom and the absence of freedom are timelessly
nonexistent in basic space.

Within awareness, a supreme state of unwavering equalness,
even as things arise, they arise naturally, holding to their own
place.
Even as they abide, they abide naturally, holding to their own
place.
Even as they are freed, they are freed naturally, holding to their
own place.

Given that awareness is unchanging and free of elaboration,
everything is of the nature of space—what arises, arises
timelessly;
what abides, abides timelessly; and what is free is free timelessly.

Thoughts arise, abide, and are freed.
Their simultaneous arising and being freed is uninterrupted.
Since it is uninterrupted, there is no separation into cause
and effect.
Since there is no cause and effect, the abyss of samsara has
been crossed.
Since there is no longer an abyss, where could one go astray?

The expanse of Samantabhadra is timelessly unchanging.
The expanse of Vajrasattva is without transition or change.
The term "buddhahood" is nothing more than a label
for what is simply recognition of the very essence of being—
the way of abiding.

With the realization of this, there are no phenomena to accept
or reject,

ཐམས་ཅད་ཆོས་ཉིད་གཅིག་ཏུ་ཕྱམ་གདལ་བ། །གསེར་གླིང་ལྟ་བུར་དབྱེ་བསལ་མེད་པ་ཡིན། །མཐའ་ཡིས་མ་རེག་གོལ་སྒྲིབ་གདར་ཤ་ཆོད། །གཡང་ས་མེད་པའི་བྱང་ཆུབ་སེམས་ཉིད་ལ། །འབད་རྩོལ་མེད་པའི་སྐུ་གསུམ་ལྷུན་རྫོགས་ཀྱང་། །བསམ་བརྗོད་འདས་ཤེས་མིང་ཙམ་བརྗོད་པར་ཟད།

།སྣང་བ་རྒྱ་ཡན་རིག་པ་རང་བྱུང་གསལ། །མ་བསྒྲིབས་ཕྱི་ནང་མེད་པར་ཟང་ཐལ་བས། །མ་བཅོས་རྣལ་གཞག་ཆོས་ཉིད་ཆེན་པོར་གསལ། །བློ་བདེའི་མལ་ན་ལུས་སེམས་ཁོང་གློད་དེ། །ཤེས་པ་བག་ཡངས་བྱར་མེད་སྐྱེས་བུ་བཞིན། །སྒྲིམས་གློད་མེད་པར་ལུས་སེམས་གང་བདེར་ཞོག

།ཇི་ལྟར་འདུག་ཀྱང་རང་གི་ངང་ལ་འདུག །ཇི་ལྟར་གནས་ཀྱང་རང་གི་ངང་ལ་གནས། །ཇི་ལྟར་འགྲོ་ཡང་རང་གི་ངང་ལ་འགྲོ། །བྱང་ཆུབ་དབྱིངས་ལ་འགྲོ་འོང་དང་གིས་མེད། །འགྲོ་འོང་མེད་པ་རྒྱལ་བ་རྣམས་ཀྱི་སྐུ།

།ཇི་ལྟར་སྨྲས་ཀྱང་རང་གི་ངང་ལ་སྨྲ། །ཇི་ལྟར་བརྗོད་ཀྱང་རང་གི་ངང་ལ་བརྗོད། །བྱང་ཆུབ་སེམས་ལ་སྨྲ་བརྗོད་དང་གིས་མེད། །སྨྲ་བརྗོད་མེད་པ་དུས་གསུམ་རྒྱལ་བའི་གསུང་།

so all things are in a state of infinite evenness that is their sole
true nature.
As on the Isle of Gold, there is no division or exclusion.
This nature is not subject to limitation, for error and obscuration
have been seen through.
Within awakened mind itself, in which there are no pitfalls,
the three kayas, involving no effort, are spontaneously perfect,
so the phrase "beyond imagination or expression" is a mere
figure of speech.

Sensory appearances are unrestricted;
awareness is evident and naturally occurring.
Since the genuine state of uncontrived rest is unobscured and
unobstructed, with no division into outer and inner,
it is evident as the supreme nature of phenomena.
Let your mind and body relax deeply in a carefree state.
With an easygoing attitude, like a person who has nothing
more to do,
let your mind and body rest in whatever way is comfortable,
neither tense nor loose.

However things stay, they stay within their fundamental nature.
However they dwell, they dwell within their fundamental nature.
However they move, they move within their fundamental nature.
Fundamentally, there is no coming or going within the basic
space of enlightenment.
The enlightened forms of victorious ones do not come or go.

However description occurs, it occurs within its fundamental
nature.
However expression occurs, it occurs within its fundamental
nature.
Fundamentally, there is no description or expression within
awakened mind.
The enlightened speech of the victorious ones of the three times
is indescribable and inexpressible.

།ཇི་ལྟར་བསམས་ཀྱང་རང་གི་ངང་ལ་བསམ། །ཇི་ལྟར་རྟོག་ཀྱང་རང་གི་ངང་ལ་རྟོག །བྱང་ཆུབ་སེམས་ལ་བསམ་རྟོག་ཡེ་ནས་མེད། །བསམ་རྟོག་བྲལ་བ་དུས་གསུམ་རྒྱལ་བའི་ཐུགས།

།མེད་ལ་ཅིར་ཡང་འབྱུང་བ་སྤྲུལ་པའི་སྐུ། །ཉིད་ལ་ཉིད་ལོངས་སྤྱོད་པ་ལོངས་སྤྱོད་རྫོགས། །དེ་ལ་དངོས་གཞི་མེད་པས་ཆོས་སྐུ་སྟེ། །འབྲས་བུ་སྐུ་གསུམ་ལྷུན་གྱིས་གྲུབ་པའི་ཀློང་།

།བྱང་ཆུབ་སེམས་ཀྱི་ཀློང་ཆེན་ངང་ཉིད་ལས། །དྲན་པའི་རྣམ་པར་རྟོག་པ་མི་འབྱུང་སྟེ། །ཤེས་པའི་མཚན་མ་ཡིད་ལ་མི་གཡོ་ན། །དེ་ཉིད་སངས་རྒྱས་ཉག་གཅིག་དགོངས་པ་ཡིན།

།བྱང་ཆུབ་རང་བཞིན་ནམ་མཁའི་དཀྱིལ་ཡངས་འདྲ། །དྲན་དང་རྟོག་པ་མེད་པ་སྒོམ་པའི་མཆོག །རང་གི་རང་བཞིན་མ་གཡོས་བཅོས་པ་མེད།། མི་བསམ་ཡིད་ལ་བྱེད་པ་རྣམ་བྲལ་བ། །རང་བབས་ཆོས་ཉིད་དུས་གསུམ་འཕོ་འགྱུར་མེད། །འགྱུ་འཕྲོའི་ཀུན་རྟོག་མེད་པ་སྒོམ་པའི་མཆོག

།དེ་བཞིན་ཉིད་དེར་གང་གནས་དམ་པའི་སེམས། །སངས་རྒྱས་ཉག་གཅིག་མཆོན་པ་ཀུན་དང་བྲལ། །

However thinking occurs, it occurs within its fundamental
nature.
However conceptualization occurs, it occurs within its
fundamental nature.
There is never any thinking or conceptualizing within awakened
mind.
The enlightened mind of the victorious ones of the three times
is free of thinking and conceptualizing.

Since what is nonexistent can occur in any way at all, there
is nirmanakaya.
Since the richness of being enjoys itself, there is sambhogakaya.
Since no substantial basis for these two exists, there is
dharmakaya.
The fruition is the expanse within which the three kayas are
spontaneously present.

Within the very state that is the vast expanse of awakened mind,
the concepts of ordinary thinking do not occur.
If the characteristics of ordinary consciousness do not stir in
the mind,
that itself is enlightened intent, the unique state of buddhahood.

The nature of enlightenment is similar to the spacious vault
of the sky.
The most sublime form of meditation involves no recollection
or thinking.
One's nature is unwavering and uncontrived.
Unplanned and completely free of the formation of ideas, the
true nature of phenomena, the naturally settled state,
is without transition or change throughout the three times.
The most sublime form of meditation involves no stirring
or proliferation of all-consuming thoughts.

Any abiding in suchness is the sacred state of mind—
the unique state of buddhahood, free of all characterization.

མི་གཡོ་ཆོས་དབྱིངས་འཛིན་རྟོག་ཕྱམ་འདས་པ། །རྒྱལ་བའི་དགོངས་
ཀློང་རང་བཞིན་ཡངས་པའི་མཆོག །ལུས་སེམས་བཅོས་པའི་འཆིང་བ་
རྣམས་སྒྲུངས་ཤིང་། །གྲིན་འདར་ལྷོད་ཆགས་དྲན་བསམ་ཅི་འགྱུས་ཀྱང་།།
གཞི་གཞག་ཆོས་ཉིད་དང་ལས་མི་གཡོ་ན། །ཐམས་ཅད་ཀུན་བཟང་
དགོངས་ཀློང་ཡངས་པ་ཡིན།

།མ་བཟུང་མ་བཏང་འཕྱར་བུའི་སྒྲིམས་གློད་མེད། །ཇི་བཞིན་རང་བབས་
རྒྱ་ཡན་དང་གིས་ཟིན། །མི་གཡོ་ཕྱམ་གདལ་ཡངས་དོག་མེད་པའི་
ཀློང་། །དྲན་བསམ་ཐམས་ཅད་རང་བྱུང་རང་ཞི་ན། །རྡོ་རྗེ་སེམས་
དཔའ་ནམ་མཁའི་དགོངས་པ་ཡིན།

།མ་བཅོས་ཀློང་དུ་མ་ཡེངས་དང་ལྡན་ན། །དྲན་རྟོག་ཡུལ་ལ་འཇུག་
པའང་ཆོས་ཉིད་དང་། །ཆེད་དུ་འཕྱར་བུས་བཅོས་ན་ཆོས་ཉིད་ཀྱང་། །
མི་རྟོག་མཁའ་ལྟར་ཡངས་ཀྱང་མཚན་མའི་གཟེབ། །ཉིན་མཚན་སྒོམ་
པས་འདའ་ཡང་འཆིང་ཞེན་ཉིད། །བསམ་གཏན་ལྷ་དང་མཚུངས་པར་
རྒྱལ་བས་གསུངས། །

It is the unwavering basic space of phenomena, a state of
evenness that transcends reifying concepts.
This is the expanse of the enlightened intent of the
victorious ones,
the sublime, spacious nature of being.
When the bonds of physical and mental contrivance
are abandoned,
there is unfeigned relaxation.
No matter what recollection stirs in the mind,
if you do not waver from the context of the true nature of
phenomena—that of resting in the ground of being—
everything is the spacious expanse of the enlightened intent
of Samantabhadra.

Since nothing is reified or discarded, there is none of the tension
or laxity of the compulsive mind.
The unrestricted state of natural settling, just as it is, is ensured
as a matter of course.
Unwavering, infinite evenness is an expanse with no fixed
dimension.
If all ordinary thinking occurs naturally and is pacified naturally,
that is the skylike enlightened intent of Vajrasattva.

If you maintain an undistracted state within the uncontrived
expanse of being,
even engaging in thoughts concerning sense objects is within
the scope of the true nature of phenomena.
As for that true nature, it is nonconceptual and as spacious
as the sky,
but if you try to contrive it deliberately and compulsively,
it becomes a cage of characteristics.
Though you may spend day and night in such meditation,
that is the bondage of fixation, pure and simple.
The Victorious One stated that it resembles the meditative
stability of the gods.

དེ་བས་མ་ཡེངས་འབད་རྩོལ་ཞིག་པའི་སེམས། །རང་བབས་འཛིན་རྩོལ་འདས་པ་ཤིན་ཏུ་གཅེས།

།རང་བྱུང་ཡེ་ཤེས་ཕྱོགས་དང་རིས་མེད་པས། །འདི་ཞེས་མི་མཚོན་རང་བཞིན་སྤྲོས་ཀུན་ཞི། །དེ་བས་ཡིད་ལ་བྱེད་པ་རྣམས་སྤངས་ཏེ། །གཞི་བྲལ་ཡངས་པ་ཆེན་པོའི་དོན་ལ་བསླབ།

།ཆོས་ཉིད་ཉག་གཅིག་རང་བྱུང་ཡེ་ཤེས་ཏེ། །ལྟ་བ་ཉག་གཅིག་སྤྲོས་པའི་མཐའ་དང་བྲལ། །སྒོམ་པ་ཉག་གཅིག་བདང་གཞག་འགྲོ་འོང་མེད། །སྤྱོད་པ་ཉག་གཅིག་བླང་དོར་གཉིས་སུ་མེད། །འབྲས་བུ་ཉག་གཅིག་སྤངས་ཐོབ་གཉིས་དང་བྲལ། །འདི་ནི་རང་བྱུང་ལྷུན་གྲུབ་དགོངས་པ་ཡིན།

།སྣང་སྲིད་སྣོད་བཅུད་འཁོར་དང་མྱ་ངན་འདས། །ཆོས་སོ་ཅོག་ཀུན་ཆོས་ཉིད་གདོད་མའི་ངང་། །རང་བྱུང་ཡེ་ཤེས་ཉིད་ལས་མ་གཡོས་པས། །གང་ཡང་གཞི་གཞག་དགོངས་པར་ཤེས་པར་བྱ།

།སྣ་ཚོགས་ཡུལ་དུ་སྣང་བའི་ཆོས་རྣམས་ལ། །གང་དུ་འདི་ལྟར་འཛོག་ཅེས་མི་རྟོག་པར། རང་བབས་སྤྲོ་བསྒྱུ་བྲལ་བར་ལྷུན་གྱིས་ཞོག །

Therefore, it is extremely crucial that your mind—
which is undistracted and in which effort and striving have
been eradicated—
settle naturally, beyond reifying effort.

Since naturally occurring timeless awareness is without
limitation or bias,
it cannot be characterized as some "thing," for all elaboration
naturally subsides.
Therefore, give up creating more concepts.
Train in the ultimate meaning of supreme spaciousness free of
any foundation.

The unique nature of phenomena is naturally occurring
timeless awareness.
The unique view is freedom from the limitations of elaboration.
In the unique meditation, nothing is discarded or adopted,
nothing comes or goes.
In the unique conduct, there is no duality of acceptance and
rejection.
The unique fruition is free of the duality of renunciation and
attainment.
This is the enlightened intent of naturally occurring spontaneous
presence.

The true nature of all phenomena in their entirety—the universe
of appearances and possibilities,
whether of samsara or nirvana—is the primordial state.
Since it does not stray from naturally occurring timeless
awareness itself,
understand it to be enlightened intent, with everything at rest
in the ground of being.

Concerning phenomena that manifest as myriad sense objects,
without thinking in any way, "This is how to rest,"
rest spontaneously in the naturally settled state, free of the
proliferation and resolution of thoughts.

ཆོས་ཉིད་མཉམ་པའི་ཀློང་དུ་དང་གིས་གནས།

།དཀར་དམར་ཡུལ་དུ་སྣང་བའི་རྣམ་པ་ལ། །དབང་པོ་མི་བསྒྱུ་མིག་ཀྱང་མི་འགྱུལ་བས། །བདག་ལ་མི་བསམ་གཞན་ལ་མི་རྟོག་པར། །ཕྱམ་ཕྱལ་ཡངས་པ་ཆེན་པོར་རང་གསལ་ཞོག

།རྒྱུ་བསྐྱེད་དཔངས་བསྟོད་སྤྲོ་བསྡུ་བྲལ་བའི་སེམས། །ཀུན་མཉམ་རང་བྱུང་ཡེ་ཤེས་དགོངས་པ་ལ། །ཕྱི་ནང་བར་མེད་ནམ་མཁའ་འདྲེས་པའི་ཉམས། །བདེ་གསལ་སྤྲོས་དང་བྲལ་བའི་ཏིང་འཛིན་འཆར།

།གཞི་གཞག་མི་གཡོ་ཆོས་ཉིད་དགོངས་པ་ལ། །ཕྱི་དང་ནང་མེད་གཟུང་འཛིན་སྤྲོས་དང་བྲལ། །ཡུལ་ཞེས་གཞན་དུ་ཞེན་པའི་སེམས་མེད་པས།། གཟུང་བའི་ཆོས་མེད་སྟོད་བཙུད་སྣང་ཞེན་བྲལ། །འཁོར་བར་སྐྱེ་བའི་ཡུལ་མེད་ནམ་མཁའ་འདྲ།

།རང་ཞེས་སེམས་ལ་ནང་དུ་མི་རྟོག་པས། །འཛིན་པའི་ཆོས་མེད་སྲིད་པའི་ཀུན་རྟོག་ཞི། །འཁོར་བར་སྐྱེ་བའི་མཁན་པོ་རྩད་ནས་ཆོད། །དེ་ཚེ་མཁའ་འདྲ་ཕྱི་ནང་འབྲུལ་པའི་ཆོས། །གང་ཡང་མི་དམིགས་ཆོས་སྐུའི་དགོངས་པར་ཕྱིན། །

Abide as a matter of course within the expanse of equalness,
the true nature of phenomena.

Neither focusing your senses on, nor letting your gaze wander to,
the manifestations of sensory appearances in all their variety,
neither thinking of "self" nor conceiving of "other,"
rest, naturally lucid, in the supremely spacious state of complete openness.

Given the enlightened intent of naturally occurring timeless awareness, in which everything is equal—
expansive and elevated mind free of the proliferation and resolution of thoughts—
the experience of blending with space, without any division into outer and inner or in between,
arises as meditative absorption that is blissful, clear, and free of elaboration.

Given the enlightened intent of the true nature of phenomena, which never strays from a state of rest, the ground of being,
there is no division into outer and inner, for that nature is free of the elaborations of dualistic perception.
There is no ordinary mind fixating on something "other"— a "sense object"—
so nothing is reified as an object, and your perceptions of the universe are free of fixation.
No context exists for taking rebirth in samsara—this is similar to space.

There is no inner concept of mind as "self,"
so nothing is reified as a subject, and the all-consuming thought patterns of conditioned existence are stilled.
The potential for rebirth in samsara is cut through at the root.
At that point, you have arrived at the enlightened intent of dharmakaya,
like space, in which there is no division into outer and inner and no frame of reference for phenomena based on confusion.

ཟད་པའི་སར་ཐུག་འགྲོ་དང་འོང་མེད་པས། །ཐམས་ཅད་ཀློང་འབྱམས་
ཀུན་ཏུ་བཟང་པོའི་ཞིང་། །ཆོས་སྐུའི་ཕོ་བྲང་མཆོག་ཏུ་ཕྱིན་པ་ཡིན།

།ད་ལྟའི་རིག་པ་གཞི་ལས་མ་གཡོས་ན། །དེ་ཉིད་གོམས་ཚས་ཕྱི་མའི་
སྲིད་པ་སྟོངས། །ཡང་སྲིད་ལེན་པའི་ལས་དང་བག་ཆགས་བྲལ། །རྒྱུ་
འབྲས་ལ་ཟློས་འཁོར་འདས་མཉམ་པར་བརྗོད། །སྲིད་ཞིར་མི་གནས་
བྱང་ཆུབ་སྙིང་པོར་ཕྱིན། །འདིར་ཡང་ཞི་གནས་རྩེ་གཅིག་ཕྱེད་པ་གཅིས།།
རང་བཞིན་རྫོགས་པ་ཆེན་པོའི་དགོངས་པ་ཡིན།

།ངང་ལས་གཡོས་ན་ཡིད་དཔྱོད་འཁོར་བ་ཉིད། །དེ་ལ་རྒྱུ་འབྲས་ཉིད་དེ་
ལ་མ་ཟློས། །ནོར་བའི་སྐྱེ་བོ་འོག་ནས་འོག་ཏུ་འགྲོ། །དེས་ན་མཆོག་
གསང་རྫོགས་པ་ཆེན་པོ་ནི། །དབྱིངས་ལས་མ་གཡོས་རྩལ་རྣམས་
གཞི་ལ་འཁྱིལ། །དགོངས་པ་མི་གཡོ་མཉམ་པར་གནས་པ་ཡིན།

།འདི་ཡི་ངང་ལ་རྒྱུ་འབྲས་བྱ་རྩོལ་མེད། །ལྟ་བ་བསྒོམ་དུ་མེད་པ་ལ་
སོགས་ཏེ། །མཐའ་དབུས་གཉིས་མེད་འགོག་པའི་ཚུལ་བརྗོད་ཀྱི། །

You have touched on the point of resolution, and since there is no coming or going,
everything is an infinite expanse, the pure realm of Samantabhadra.
You have reached the sublime palace of dharmakaya.

If awareness in the moment does not stray from the ground of being,
familiarization with that experience negates any furthering of conditioned existence.
You are free of the karma and habitual patterns that perpetuate rebirth.
You have come to the decisive experience of causality, described as the equalness of samsara and nirvana.
You have arrived at the heart essence of enlightenment, which does not abide in conditioned existence or the state of peace.
It is crucial that you distinguish between this and a one-pointed state of calm abiding.
This is the enlightened intent of natural great perfection.

If you stray from your fundamental nature, the functioning of conceptual mind is samsara, pure and simple.
It involves cause and effect—you have not come to the decisive experience.
A person who makes this mistake falls lower and lower.
Therefore, the sublime secret—great perfection—does not stray from basic space,
and the expressions of dynamic energy resolve within the ground of being.
Enlightened intent abides as an unwavering state of equalness.

Within this context, there is no cause and effect, no concerted effort.
View, for example, cannot be cultivated in meditation.
Although the mode of cessation is described as having neither center nor limit,

གཞན་དུ་ངང་ལས་ཕྱིར་འཕྲུལ་རྩལ་ཉིད་ལ། །རོལ་པ་སྣ་ཚོགས་སྣང་
སྲིད་དགུ་འཆར་བས། །རྒྱུ་འབྲས་མེད་ཅེས་ནམ་ཡང་མ་བརྗོད་ཅིག

།རྟེན་འབྲེལ་རྐྱེན་འབྱུང་འདུས་བྱས་གྲངས་བསམ་འདས། །འཁོར་བའི་
འཕྲུལ་སྣང་ཞི་བདེའང་གྲངས་བསམ་འདས། །དེ་ཀུན་རྒྱུ་རྐྱེན་ཚོགས་
པའི་རྟེན་འབྲེལ་ཉིད།

།གཉིས་ལ་གཞལ་ན་གང་ཡང་མ་གྲུབ་ལྟར། །ལམ་དུ་བྱེད་པས་གཉིས་
ཐོག་མི་གཡོའི་དུས། །གང་ཡང་མི་དམིགས་དགོངས་པའི་དུས་ན་རྩི། །
གཉིས་ཐོག་མཐར་ཕྱིན་གང་ཡང་གོས་མི་འགྱུར།

།ཉོན་མོངས་ལས་དང་བག་ཆགས་གློང་ཆེན་འདི། །རྟེན་མེད་སྒྱུ་མའི་
སྤྲུལ་པའི་རྩེད་མོ་བྱེད། །འདི་ལས་ཐར་དགོས་རྒྱུ་འབྲས་ལ་བློས་འཚལ།།
དོ་ཡི་ཐབས་ནི་འདི་ལས་མཆོག་གཞན་མེད། །དེ་ཕྱིར་ཆོས་ཉིད་དགོངས་
པ་མ་གཡོས་གཅིས། །འདི་ཉིད་ཁོ་བོའི་སྙིང་གདམ་ཟབ་མོའི་གློང་། །

when dynamic energy itself deviates from this natural state,
the myriad display arises as the multiplicity of the universe of appearances and possibilities.
So never say categorically, "There is no cause and effect."

Interdependence ensures that conditioned, composite phenomena are beyond enumeration and imagination.
Confused perception in samsara, and even states of peace and bliss, are beyond enumeration and imagination.
All of this constitutes the very process of interdependence, which is the coming together of causes and conditions.

If you evaluate your fundamentally unconditioned nature,
you find it has never existed as anything whatsoever.
So too, in taking this as your path, you have no frame of reference whatsoever
for straying from that fundamentally unconditioned nature in all its immediacy.
Rather, you appreciate it within the context of enlightened intent.
Having reached the ultimate state in the immediacy of your fundamentally unconditioned nature,
you are not sullied by anything at all.

Afflictive emotions, karma, and habitual patterns have no support
within this vast expanse, but are the playing out of magical games of illusion.
You must be liberated from this, so please come to a decisive experience of causality.
As a means of doing so, there is nothing superior to this approach.
Therefore, it is crucial not to stray from the enlightened intent of the true nature of phenomena.
This is the expanse of my profound and heartfelt advice.

ཀུན་ཡིན་ཀུན་མིན་ཡིན་མིན་འདས་པ་གཅིས།

།ཆོས་དབྱིངས་རིན་པོ་ཆེའི་མཛོད་ལས། །དགོངས་པ་ཆོས་ཉིད་ལས་མི་གཡོ་བར་བསྟན་པའི་ལེའུ་སྟེ་བཅུ་པའོ།།

།།ཐམས་ཅད་མཁའ་མཉམ་བྱང་ཆུབ་སེམས་གཅིག་ལ། །གཉིས་སུ་བཟུང་བས་རྒྱུ་འབྲས་སྲིད་པར་འཁྲུལ། །འཁྲུལ་སྣང་རྟེན་མེད་སྒྱུ་མའི་སྣང་བ་ལ། །ཐུག་ཕྲད་རྗེས་མེད་རྩིས་གདབ་བྲལ་བར་སྒྲོངས།

།མི་འདོད་ཐོག་ཏུ་བབ་ལ་དོར་བྱའི་སེམས། །ཁྲོ་དང་མི་དགའ་ཕྲག་དོག་འཁྲུག་དང་འཚིག །སྐྱོ་བའི་ཡིད་དབྱུང་ན་ཚ་སྡུག་བསྔལ་སེམས། །འཆི་དང་སྐྲག་བས་འཇིགས་ལ་སོགས་པ་སྟེ། །རྩལ་ལས་རོལ་པར་ཤར་དུས་ངོས་བཟུང་ལ། །མི་སྤོང་མི་ལེན་མི་སྒྲུབ་མི་སྒྱུར་ཞིང་། །མི་ལྟ་མི་སྒོམ་རང་བབས་ཕྱམ་གཅིག་ཏུ། །དམིགས་བསམ་སྤྲོ་བསྡུ་བྲལ་བར་ལྷུན་གྱིས་ཞོག །རྗེས་མེད་རང་ཡལ་མཁའ་ཀློང་དག་པའི་སེམས། །གསལ་དངས་ངར་དང་བཅས་པ་ཁོང་ནས་འཆར།

།ཡིན་མིན་མེད་པའི་རིག་པ་ཕྱོགས་ཡན་ལ། །

It is crucial to go beyond what everything is or is not,
transcending "is" and "is not."

This is the tenth section of *The Precious Treasury of the Basic Space of Phenomena,* demonstrating that enlightened intent does not deviate from the true nature of phenomena.

❖

WITHIN THE ONENESS of everything as awakened mind, equal to space,
dualistic perception draws you into confusion—conditioned existence and causality.
Since sensory appearances based on confusion are illusory and have no true support,
when you encounter them directly, maintain the experience of their leaving no trace, free of evaluation.

When something unwanted falls into your lap, you have a negative reaction,
such as anger, dislike, envy, upset, irritation, anxiety,
depression, mental anguish, or fear of death and rebirth.
When such reactions arise as a display due to dynamic energy, identify them as such.
Do not renounce them, indulge in them, refine them away, transform them, look at them, or meditate on them.
Rather, rest spontaneously in the single, naturally settled state of evenness,
free of the proliferation and resolution of conceptual frameworks.
Mind as a pure expanse of space, in which things vanish naturally and leave no trace,
arises with intensity from within, pristinely lucid.

Within unconstrained awareness, which neither "is" nor "is not,"

འདིར་གདོད་མེད་པའི་སྣང་བ་ཐུག་ཕྲད་ཀྱིས། །འདིར་བཟུང་མེད་པའི་ངང་དེར་རང་གཞག་པས། །འདིར་གྲོལ་མེད་པའི་དགག་སྒྲུབ་རྗེས་མེད་ཡལ། །འཛིན་ཞེན་མེད་པའི་ཉམས་མྱོང་ཁོང་རྡོལ་འབྱུང་། །འདི་ཉིད་ཇི་བཞིན་དགོངས་ཀློང་ཡེ་ནས་ཡངས།

།དེ་བཞིན་འདོད་ཅིང་ཡིད་ལ་དགའ་བའི་སེམས། །གྲུབ་བདེ་གཉེན་དང་གཏམ་སྙན་ལོངས་སྤྱོད་དང་། །གནས་དང་ཕྱོགས་ནི་ཡིད་དུ་འོང་བ་དེར། །རང་བཞིན་དགའ་བས་བརྒྱན་པའི་སེམས་ཤར་བ། །དེ་ཉིད་ངོས་བཟུང་རང་བབས་ཅོག་གཞག་གིས། །གདོད་མའི་དབྱིངས་སུ་མ་བཅོས་ལྷུན་གྱིས་གྲུབ།

།རང་བཞིན་བར་མ་འགྲོ་འདུག་གྱིན་འདར་གནས། །དགའ་དང་མི་དགའ་གཉིས་མིན་ཅི་ཤར་ཡང་། །ཤར་དུས་ངོས་བཟུང་སྤང་བླང་མ་བྱས་པས།། རང་བབས་ཆོས་ཉིད་དབྱེ་བསལ་མེད་པ་ནི། །གཏི་མུག་འོད་གསལ་ཆེན་པོར་གྲོལ་ཞེས་བྱ།

།མཚན་མོ་ལ་སོགས་གཉིད་ཀྱིས་མྱོས་པ་ནའང་། །རང་བབས་སྒྲོ་བསྐུ་བྲལ་བའི་ངང་ཉལ་བས། །རགས་པར་སྣང་བ་ནུབ་པས་དེར་འཛིན་ནུབ།།

sensory appearances are not fixated on as anything, but rather are encountered directly.
This brings about natural rest in the state that cannot be reified as anything,
and suppression and indulgence, which are not anything that can be freed in some way,
fade without leaving a trace.
An experience without fixation wells up from within.
This itself—just as it is—is the timelessly spacious expanse of enlightened intent.

Similarly, you may experience what is desirable and brings joy to the mind—
things accomplished with ease, friends, pleasant news, wealth to be enjoyed, and attractive places and regions.
With anything attractive, there arises a state of mind that is naturally enriched by joy.
When you identify this and rest imperturbably, settling naturally,
you experience it as uncontrived and spontaneously present in primordial basic space.

You may have a neutral attitude—when you are going about or sitting or resting quite indifferently—
that is neither pleasant nor unpleasant.
Regardless of what arises, identify its nature as it arises, without reacting positively or negatively.
Thus, the true nature of phenomena, the naturally settled state without differentiation or exclusion,
is called "ignorance free as supreme utter lucidity."

At night and other times when you are overtaken by sleep,
as you lie in a naturally settled state free of the proliferation and resolution of thoughts,
sensory appearances that manifest in obvious ways disappear, so reification of them disappears as well.

ཕྲ་བ་ཆེས་ཕྲ་འཛིན་པར་བཅས་ནུབ་པས། །ཆ་མཉམ་མི་རྟོག་ངང་དུ་རིག་པའི་སེམས། །འབྱུང་འཇུག་རེ་དོགས་བྲལ་བར་རང་བཞིན་གནས། །ཀུན་རྟོག་ཆོས་དབྱིངས་གྲོལ་བའི་དུས་ཡིན་པས། །འཁོར་བ་མྱང་འདས་གྲོལ་ཞེས་བརྗོད་པ་ཡིན།

།གཉིད་ཀྱང་རང་བྱུང་གདོད་མའི་ཀློང་ཆེན་ཏེ། །རྩལ་རྣམས་ངོ་བོའི་དབྱིངས་སུ་གཞིར་ཐིམ་པས། །རོལ་པར་འཛིན་པའི་སྤྲོས་ཀུན་ངང་གིས་ཞི། །ཟུར་མེད་རང་བྱུང་ཡེ་ཤེས་དགོངས་པའོ།

།དེ་ལྟར་འདོད་དང་མི་འདོད་བར་མའི་སེམས། །དུག་གསུམ་རྩལ་ལས་རོལ་པར་ཤར་ཏོ་ཅོག །དབྱིངས་ལས་བྱུང་ཞིང་དབྱིངས་ཀྱི་ངང་དུ་ཤར། །དབྱིངས་སུ་མ་གཏོགས་གཡོས་པ་འགའ་མེད་པས། །གཟེད་དང་བཅོས་བསྒྱུར་གང་ཡང་མི་བྱེད་པར། །དབྱིངས་ཉིད་ངོས་གཟུང་དང་དེར་བཞག་མ་ཐག །རང་ཞི་རང་ཡལ་རང་གྲོལ་འགྲོ་བ་གནད།

།ཉོན་མོངས་ལས་དང་བག་ཆགས་ཐམས་ཅད་ཀྱང་། །རྩལ་ལས་རོལ་པར་ཤར་བའི་ཚོ་འཕྲུལ་ལ། །གཉེན་པོ་བཟང་ཐུས་ཐར་པའི་ལམ་ཉིད་ཀྱང་། །རྩལ་ལས་རོལ་པར་ཤར་བའི་ཚོ་འཕྲུལ་ཏེ། །

With the disappearance of even what is subtle or very subtle,
together with the reification of it,
the mind that is aware in a uniform, nonconceptual state
abides naturally, free of the occurrence of and involvement in
thoughts, as well as hope and fear.
This is the context in which all-consuming concepts are free
within the basic space of phenomena
and so is described as "samsara being free as nirvana."

Even sleep is the primordial vast expanse, occurring naturally.
Expressions of dynamic energy are absorbed into the ground of
being, into the basic space that is its essence,
so that all the elaborations perceived as a display subside as
a matter of course.
This is the enlightened intent of naturally occurring timeless
awareness, in which nothing need be done.

Thus, all desirable, undesirable, and neutral mental states,
in which the three poisons arise as a display due to dynamic
energy,
occur within basic space, arising within the context of that space.
Since they occur only within basic space, not straying from it in
the least,
without trying to anticipate or manipulate them in any way,
it is crucial to identify basic space itself, for as soon as you rest
in that context,
they will subside naturally, vanish naturally, and be freed
naturally.

Moreover, all afflictive emotions, karma, and habitual patterns
are magical expressions arising as a display due to dynamic
energy.
Antidotes that bring improvement—even the path to
liberation—
are magical expressions arising as a display due to dynamic
energy.

གཉིས་ཀ་རྩལ་ལས་རོལ་པར་ཡེ་ཤར་བས། །ངོ་ཤེས་དང་དུ་མ་བཅོས་འཛོག་པ་གནད། །བང་མཉམ་འགྲོས་མཉམ་གཞི་ནས་གཡོས་པར་མཉམ། །རྐྱེན་བྱུང་འདུས་བྱས་རྒྱུ་འབྲས་མ་འདས་པས། །རང་གཞག་ཅོག་གཞག་རྒྱུ་འབྲས་ཀློས་པ་གཅེས།

།འདི་ནི་མཆོག་གསང་ཐེག་པའི་ཡང་རྩེ་སྟེ། །བློ་དམན་རྣམས་ལ་མི་སྨྲ་ཤིན་ཏུ་གསང་། །སྒྲོ་སྐུར་དབང་གིས་སྙིང་པོའི་བསྟན་པ་འཆལ། །སྒྲོ་འདེབས་ཉིད་དང་དགོངས་པ་ལོག་པར་ཞུགས། །གསང་སྒྲོ་འཆོལ་རྣམས་མཐའ་མེད་ངན་འགྲོར་ལྷུང་། །དེ་བས་རབ་གསང་ཐེག་པ་རྒྱལ་པོའི་གདུང་། །སྐལ་བཟང་དམ་པ་རྣམས་ལ་བསྟན་ཞིང་གཏད།

།མདོར་ན་གང་སྣང་ཡུལ་སེམས་རྐྱེན་རྣམས་ལ། །གཉེན་པོ་མི་འཛུག་རྩོལ་བས་མ་སྤྱངས་པར། །རང་གཞག་ཅོག་གཞག་རང་བབས་རིག་པའི་གནད།

།བདེ་སྡུག་ཐམས་ཅད་རིག་པའི་འཆར་ཚུལ་ལ། །བླང་དོར་གཉིས་སུ་བཟུང་བས་སྲིད་པར་འཆིང་།

།གང་སྣང་ཡུལ་མཉམ་དབང་པོའི་ངོར་གསལ་ཙམ། །

Since both arise timelessly as a display due to this energy,
it is crucial to rest without contrivance within the state of recognition.
They are equal in mode, equal in manner, and equal in stirring from the ground of being.
They occur circumstantially, are compounded, and do not transcend causality,
so it is essential that you transcend causality—resting naturally, resting imperturbably.

This is the very pinnacle of the sublime secret approach.
Do not speak about it to those of lesser aptitude, but keep it extremely secret.
By being misinterpreted, the teachings concerning the heart essence will be distorted.
Exaggeration and underestimation are at odds with enlightened intent.
Those who violate the bounds of secrecy fall endlessly into lower states.
Therefore, the legacy of the most majestic and utterly secret spiritual approach
is taught and entrusted to holy people with good fortune.

In brief, whatever circumstance manifests—whether a sense object or state of mind—
do not apply antidotes or make an effort to abandon it,
for the key point of naturally settled awareness is to rest naturally, to rest imperturbably.

Though all pleasure and pain are ways in which awareness arises,
you are bound to conditioned existence by reifying them dualistically as things to accept or eliminate.

Whatever appearances manifest are equal as sense objects—simply what is evident to the sense faculties.

གང་ཤར་སེམས་མཉམ་དྲན་རིག་རྗེས་མེད་ཙམ། །གཉིས་ཀ་འཕྲལ་མཉམ་དགག་སྒྲུབ་འཆིང་བ་ཙམ། །དོན་ལ་ཕྱུག་མཉམ་གཞི་མེད་སྣང་བ་ཙམ། །ཡུལ་རྣམས་རིས་མཉམ་གཞིག་ན་རྗེས་མེད་ཙམ། །བློ་རྣམས་ངོར་མཉམ་དཔྱད་ན་ནམ་མཁའ་ཙམ། །ཡུལ་སེམས་གཉིས་མེད་བར་སྣང་དག་པ་ཙམ། །དེ་ལྟར་སུས་ཤེས་ཀུན་ཏུ་བཟང་པོའི་གདུང་། །རྒྱལ་བའི་སྲས་མཆོག་ས་རབ་རིག་པ་འཛིན།

།འདི་ལྟར་ཆོས་རྣམས་ཡོད་མཉམ་མེད་མཉམ་ལ། །སྣང་མཉམ་སྟོང་མཉམ་བདེན་མཉམ་རྫུན་མཉམ་པས། །སྲིད་གཉེན་འབད་རྩོལ་འཆིང་ཞེན་ཀུན་ཐོང་ལ། །ཡུལ་མེད་མཉམ་པ་ཆེན་པོར་ཕྲུམ་གདོལ་ཅིག །སེམས་མེད་རིག་པ་ཆེན་པོར་ཕྲུམ་གདོལ་ཅིག །སྐྱོན་མེད་དག་མཉམ་ཆེན་པོར་ཕྲུམ་གདོལ་ཅིག

།ཆོས་དབྱིངས་རིན་པོ་ཆེའི་མཛོད་ལས། །རྐྱེན་སྣང་མཁའ་མཉམ་དག་པར་བསྟན་པའི་ལེའུ་སྟེ་བཅུ་གཅིག་པའོ།།

།།ཆོས་ཀུན་བྱང་ཆུབ་སེམས་སུ་ཡི་གྲོལ་བས། །མ་གྲོལ་བ་ཡི་ཆོས་ནི་ཡོད་མ་ཡིན།

Whatever thoughts arise are equal as mental events—simply conscious states that leave no trace.
Both are equal in the moment—simply the bonds of denial or affirmation.
In actuality, they are equal in the final analysis—nothing but appearances that have no basis.
Sense objects are equal in their distinctness—upon examination simply leaving no trace.
Ordinary states of consciousness are equal in essence—upon analysis nothing but space.
Objects and mind are nondual—simply pure open space.
Whoever understands things in this way is a descendant of Samantabhadra—
a sublime spiritual heir of the victorious ones, a master of awareness in the highest sense.

Thus, phenomena are equally existent, equally nonexistent,
equally apparent, equally empty, equally true, and equally false,
so cast aside all antidotes that involve renunciation, all concerted effort, all binding fixation.
Expand into supreme equalness, in which sense objects do not exist.
Expand into supreme awareness, in which ordinary mind does not exist.
Expand into supreme purity and equality, in which flaws do not exist.

This is the eleventh section of *The Precious Treasury of the Basic Space of Phenomena,* demonstrating that manifest circumstances, equal to space in extent, are pure.

❖

ALL PHENOMENA are timelessly free in awakened mind,
and so there is no phenomenon that is not free.

།འཁོར་བ་ཡི་གྲོལ་གདོད་ནས་དག་པར་གྲོལ། །འདས་པ་ཡི་གྲོལ་ལྷུན་གྱིས་རྫོགས་པར་གྲོལ། །སྣང་བ་ཡི་གྲོལ་གཞི་རྩ་མེད་པར་གྲོལ། །སྲིད་པ་ཡི་གྲོལ་བྱང་ཆུབ་སྙིང་པོར་གྲོལ། །སྤྲོས་པ་ཡི་གྲོལ་སྨུ་མཐའ་མེད་པར་གྲོལ། །སྤྲོས་མེད་ཡི་གྲོལ་མ་སྐྱེས་དག་པར་གྲོལ།

།བདེ་བ་ཡི་གྲོལ་ཆོས་ཉིད་ཕྱམ་དུ་གྲོལ། །སྡུག་བསྔལ་ཡི་གྲོལ་གཞི་མཉམ་ཡངས་པར་གྲོལ། །བར་མ་ཡི་གྲོལ་མཁའ་མཉམ་ཆོས་སྐུར་གྲོལ། །དག་པ་ཡི་གྲོལ་དག་གཉིས་སྟོང་པར་གྲོལ། །མ་དག་ཡི་གྲོལ་ཡོངས་གྲོལ་ཆེན་པོར་གྲོལ།

།ས་ལམ་ཡི་གྲོལ་བསྐྱེད་རྫོགས་བྲལ་བར་གྲོལ། །ལྟ་སྒོམ་ཡི་གྲོལ་སྤང་བླང་མེད་པར་གྲོལ། །སྤྱོད་པ་ཡི་གྲོལ་ཀུན་ཏུ་བཟང་པོར་གྲོལ། །འབྲས་བུ་ཡི་གྲོལ་རེ་དོགས་མེད་པར་གྲོལ། །དམ་ཚིག་ཡི་གྲོལ་ཆོས་ཉིད་ཆེན་པོར་གྲོལ། །བཟླས་བརྗོད་ཡི་གྲོལ་གླིང་བརྗོད་བྲལ་བར་གྲོལ།། ཏིང་འཛིན་ཡི་གྲོལ་བསམ་ཡུལ་མེད་པར་གྲོལ།

།ཡོད་མེད་ཡི་གྲོལ་མཐའ་ལས་འདས་པར་གྲོལ། །

Samsara is timelessly free, free in primordial purity.
Nirvana is timelessly free, free in spontaneous perfection.
Sensory appearances are timelessly free, free in having no basis or foundation.
Conditioned existence is timelessly free, free in the heart essence of enlightenment.
Elaboration is timelessly free, free in the absence of limiting alternatives.
Nonelaboration is timelessly free, free in unborn purity.

Pleasure is timelessly free, free in the evenness that is the true nature of phenomena.
Pain is timelessly free, free in the uniform spaciousness of the ground of being.
Neutral sensations are timelessly free, free in dharmakaya, equal to space.
Purity is timelessly free, free in the emptiness of underlying purity.
Impurity is timelessly free, free in the supreme state of total freedom.

Levels of realization and spiritual paths are timelessly free, free in transcending the stages of development and completion.
View and meditation are timelessly free, free in the absence of renunciation and acceptance.
Conduct is timelessly free, free in the wholly positive state.
Fruition is timelessly free, free in the absence of hope and fear.
Samaya is timelessly free, free in the supreme nature of phenomena.
Recitation and mantra repetition are timelessly free, free in transcending verbal expression.
Meditative absorption is timelessly free, free in transcending the realm of thought.

Existence and nonexistence are timelessly free, for freedom lies in the transcendence of extremes.

རྟག་ཆད་ཡི་གྲོལ་གཞི་རྩ་མེད་པར་གྲོལ། །ཡང་དག་ཡི་གྲོལ་དམིགས་བསམ་འདས་པར་གྲོལ། །ཡང་དག་མིན་གྲོལ་ཕྱོགས་བསམ་འདས་པར་གྲོལ། །ལས་རྣམས་ཡི་གྲོལ་གོས་པ་མེད་པར་གྲོལ། །ཉོན་མོངས་ཡི་གྲོལ་འཆིང་གྲོལ་མེད་པར་གྲོལ། །བག་ཆགས་ཡི་གྲོལ་རྟེན་གཞི་མེད་པར་གྲོལ། །རྣམ་སྨིན་ཡི་གྲོལ་སྤྱོད་གཞི་མེད་པར་གྲོལ།

།གཉིས་པོ་ཡི་གྲོལ་སྤང་བྱ་མེད་པར་གྲོལ། །སྤང་བླང་གཉིས་མེད་མཁའ་མཉམ་ཡངས་པར་གྲོལ། །གྲོལ་བ་ཡི་གྲོལ་བཅིངས་པ་མེད་པར་གྲོལ། །མ་གྲོལ་ཡི་གྲོལ་བཅིང་གྲོལ་མེད་པར་གྲོལ། །བློད་པ་ཡི་གྲོལ་བློད་རྒྱུ་མེད་པར་གྲོལ། །ཅོག་གཞག་ཡི་གྲོལ་འཇོག་རྒྱུ་མེད་པར་གྲོལ།

།མདོར་ན་སྣང་ཞིང་སྲིད་པའི་ཆོས་རྣམས་དང་། །མི་སྣང་མི་སྲིད་ཆོས་ལས་འདས་སོ་ཅོག །ཐམས་ཅད་ཡི་ནས་དབྱིངས་སུ་གྲོལ་ཟིན་པས། །ད་གཟོད་འབད་པས་སུས་ཀྱང་གྲོལ་མི་དགོས།

།དེ་ལ་འབད་རྩོལ་བྱས་ཀྱང་དོན་མེད་པས། །མ་བྱེད་མ་བྱེད་རྩོལ་ཞིང་སྒྲུབ་མ་བྱེད།

།

Affirmation and denial are timelessly free, for freedom lies in
the lack of any basis or foundation.
What is authentic is timelessly free, for freedom lies in the
transcendence of conceptual frameworks.
What is not authentic is timelessly free, for freedom lies in the
transcendence of conceptual bias.
Karma is timelessly free, for freedom lies in the absence of any
sullying factors.
Afflictive emotions are timelessly free, for freedom lies in the
absence of either bondage or freedom.
Habitual patterns are timelessly free, for freedom lies in the lack
of any basis for supporting them.
The consequences of actions are timelessly free, for freedom lies
in the lack of any basis for experiencing them.

Antidotes are timelessly free, free in the absence of anything
to abandon.
There is neither renunciation nor acceptance, but freedom in
expansiveness equal to space itself.
Freedom is timelessly free, free in the absence of bondage.
The lack of freedom is timelessly free, free in the absence of both
bondage and freedom.
Relaxation is timelessly free, free in the absence of anything
to be relaxed.
The state of resting imperturbably is timelessly free, free in the
absence of anything to be brought to rest.

In brief, all phenomena that are appearances or possibilities,
as well as what is neither an appearance nor a possibility and is
beyond ordinary phenomena—
all these are already timelessly free in basic space,
so there is no need now for anyone to make an effort to free
them anew.

Even though you might make an effort to do this, it would be
pointless,
so don't! Don't! Do not strive or try to achieve!

མ་ལྟ་མ་ལྟ་ཡིད་ཀྱི་ཆོས་མ་ལྟ། །མ་བསྒོམས་མ་བསྒོམས་བློ་ཡི་ཆོས་མ་བསྒོམས། །མ་དཔྱད་མ་དཔྱད་ཡུལ་སེམས་རྗེས་མ་དཔྱད། །མ་བསྒྲུབས་མ་བསྒྲུབས་རེ་དོགས་འབྲས་མ་བསྒྲུབ། །མ་སྤྱངས་མ་སྤྱངས་ཉོན་མོངས་ལས་མ་སྤྱངས། །མ་ལེན་མ་ལེན་ཡང་དག་ཆོས་མ་ལེན། །མ་འཆིངས་མ་འཆིངས་རང་གི་རྒྱུད་མ་འཆིངས།

།ཐམས་ཅད་ཕྱམ་ལོག་གང་ལའང་ཡུལ་མེད་པས། །ཁྲིགས་དང་ཆོས་མེད་དམིགས་གཏད་ངོས་གཟུང་མེད། །གཞི་ལོག་ལམ་ལོག་འབྲས་བུའི་ཆོས་ལོག་པས། །ལེགས་ཉེས་ཞོར་གོང་རྟུལ་ཙམ་དམིགས་སུ་མེད། །ཕྱམ་ཕྱམ་ཕྱང་ཆད་ཡེ་ཆད་སྣང་སྲིད་ཆད། །འཁོར་འདས་རྡུ་ལོག་དབྱིངས་ཀྱང་སོ་ན་མེད། །གང་ཡིན་ཅི་ཡིན་འདི་ཡིན་གཏད་སོ་མེད། །ཁྱེད་ཅག་ཅི་བྱ་ང་ནི་གང་ན་འདུག །ཞོར་ཤུལ་ད་མེད་འདི་ལ་སུས་ཅི་བྱ།། ཧ་ཧ་འདི་འདྲ་མཚར་ཆེ་དགོད་རེ་བྲོ།

།སྣང་སྲིད་སྣོད་བཅུད་འཁྲུལ་པ་རྡུ་ལོག་པས། །ཉིན་མཚན་ཡི་སངས་རང་སངས་ནམ་མཁའ་སངས།

།

Don't look! Don't look! Do not look at the concepts in your
mind!
Don't meditate! Don't meditate! Do not meditate on the
phenomena of your ordinary consciousness!
Don't analyze! Don't analyze! Do not analyze sense objects and
ordinary mind!
Don't try to achieve! Don't try to achieve! Do not try to achieve
results out of hope and fear!
Don't reject! Don't reject! Do not reject afflictive emotions and
karma!
Don't accept! Don't accept! Do not accept anything as true!
Don't bind! Don't bind! Do not bind your mindstream!

Since everything reverts to a state of evenness, with no object
whatsoever existing,
there is no orderly process, there are no phenomena, there is no
identifiable frame of reference.
The ground collapses, the path collapses, and any sense of
a fruition collapses,
so you cannot conceive in the slightest of good or bad, loss
or injury.
Your experience of evenness is decisive, timelessly so,
and you feel certainty about the universe of appearances and
possibilities.
The division between samsara and nirvana collapses—not even
basic space exists innately.
There is no reference point—no "How is it?" "What is it?"
"It is this!"
What can any of you do? Where is the "I"?
What can anyone do about what was so before but now is not?
Ha! Ha! I burst out laughing at such a great marvel as this!

Since the perspective of confusion—the universe of appearances
and possibilities—collapses,
day and night are timelessly pristine, naturally pristine, pristine
in space.

ཞག་དང་ཆོས་སངས་ལོ་ཟླ་བསྐལ་པ་སངས། །གཅིག་སངས་ཀུན་སངས་ཆོས་དང་ཆོས་མིན་སངས། །འཁོར་འདས་འཁྲུལ་གཞི་གདོད་མའི་དབྱིངས་སུ་སངས། །དབྱིངས་ཞེས་ཐ་སྙད་བློ་ཡི་ཆོས་སངས་པས།། གང་སྒྲུབ་ཅི་འབད་དུ་ནི་ཅི་ཞིག་གཉེར། །འདོད་བློའི་འཁྲིས་ཟད་ནམ་མཁའ་ཡ་མཚན་ཆེ། །ཆོས་མེད་སྤྲང་པོའི་རང་བཞིན་དེ་འདྲར་ཟད།

།ས་གཞི་རིན་ཆེན་ནམ་མཁའ་བར་སྣང་སྟོང་། །རྟེན་མེད་ཡི་གྲོལ་དགོངས་པར་ལྷུན་གྲུབ་པས། །སྲིད་གསུམ་སྣོད་བཅུད་ཡུལ་མེད་ཆེན་པོར་གྲོལ།

།ཕྱོགས་མེད་ཕྱོགས་སུ་འཛིན་པས་བཅིངས་པ་རྣམས། །རང་བཞིན་མ་ཤེས་རང་གིས་རང་བསླད་པས། །རང་ལ་རང་སྣོང་འཁྲུལ་པ་ཨ་རེ་འཁྲུལ། །འཁྲུལ་པ་མེད་ལ་གཡང་སར་འཛིན་པས་འཁྲུལ།

།འཁྲུལ་དང་མ་འཁྲུལ་བྱང་ཆུབ་སེམས་ཀྱི་ཀློང་། །བྱང་ཆུབ་སེམས་ལ་འཁྲུལ་གྲོལ་ཡི་ནས་མེད། །དེ་ལས་རོལ་པར་ཤར་ལ་འཛིན་པས་བཅིངས། །དོན་ལ་འཆིང་གྲོལ་གཉིས་མེད་ཡུལ་སེམས་མེད། །མེད་ལ་ཡོད་པར་འཛིན་པས་མ་བསླུ་ཅིག

Days and dates are pristine; months, years, and eons are pristine.
One thing is pristine; everything is pristine.
The spiritual and the nonspiritual are pristine.
Samsara, nirvana, and the ground of confusion are pristine in primordial basic space.
The term "basic space," a product of conventional mind, is pristine.
However you strive, whatever effort you make, what now will be of value?
The entanglements of the desiring mind resolve—the supreme marvel of space!
The nature of this irreligious beggar resolved into such a state.

The fortresses of the foundation, of jewels, and of surrounding space
are spontaneously present within enlightened intent, which is timelessly free in that it has no underlying basis,
so the universe of the three states of conditioned existence is free within the supreme state in which no sense objects exist.

Those who bind themselves by holding to biases where none exist
do not understand the nature of being.
They themselves corrupt themselves.
They themselves delude themselves.
They are confused—so confused!
They are confused by their perception of an abyss where no confusion exists.

Whether or not there is confusion, there is the expanse of awakened mind.
There is never any confusion or freedom in awakened mind.
You are bound by reifying what arises from it as a display.
In actuality, there is neither bondage nor freedom.
Neither sense objects nor ordinary mind exist.
Do not be seduced into believing in the existence of what does not exist.

།ཡེ་སངས་རྒྱས་པས་གྲོལ་བའི་རིག་པ་དེ། །གཏད་འཛིན་ཆོས་ཀྱི་གཟེབ་ཏུ་མ་འཆིངས་ཤིག །ཡེ་ནས་ཡུལ་མེད་རྣམ་ཀུན་དག་པའི་ཀློང་། །མཁའ་མཉམ་བདེ་ཆེན་གཞི་རྩ་བྱང་ཆུབ་ཀློང་། །དེ་ལ་འཁོར་བ་མི་སྲིད་གདོད་མའི་བབས།

།ཐིག་ལེ་ཉག་གཅིག་སྒྲ་ཟུར་མེད་པ་ལ། །གཅིག་དང་ཐ་དད་འཛིན་པ་འཁྲུལ་པའི་སེམས། །རང་བྱུང་ཡེ་ཤེས་རྒྱུ་རྐྱེན་མེད་པ་ལ། །འཁོར་བའི་ལམ་དུ་འཛིན་པ་བྱང་ཆུབ་གེགས། །ལྷུན་གྲུབ་ཕྱོགས་མེད་མཐའ་དང་བྲལ་བ་ལ། །ཕྱོགས་ལྟའི་མཐའ་ལ་ཞེན་པ་སྒོམ་བྱེད་བདུད། །དངོས་མཚན་མེད་པའི་སྟོང་པ་འགག་མེད་ལ། །ཡོད་མེད་སྣང་སྟོང་འདོགས་པ་ལོག་པའི་བློ། །དེས་ན་གང་འདོད་ཕྱོགས་རིས་གཟེབ་བོར་ལ། །ལྷུན་གྲུབ་ཕྱོགས་མེད་ནམ་མཁའ་ལྟར་ཤེས་བྱོས།

།སྣང་གྲགས་མཐོང་ཐོས་ཚོགས་དྲུག་ཅི་ཤར་ཡང་། །ཐམས་ཅད་རང་གསལ་དབྱེ་བསལ་མེད་པའི་ཀློང་། །ཡེ་གྲོལ་མཉམ་པའི་ཀློང་དུ་ལ་ཟློས་ཤིག

Awareness is free in that it is timelessly awakened buddhahood.
Do not confine it within the trap of the ordinary mind of reifying fixation.
The completely pure expanse in which objects never exist
is the expanse of awakened mind, the supremely blissful ground equal to space.
Samsara is not possible within that context, which abides primordially and innately.

Given that the unique sphere of being is without edges or corners,
to hold that things are the same or different is the confusion of ordinary mind.
Given that naturally occurring timeless awareness has neither cause nor condition,
perceiving it to be involved in the samsaric process is a hindrance to enlightenment.
Given that unbiased spontaneous presence is free of limitation,
fixation on the limitations of biased views is the mara that creates complacency.
Given that unceasing emptiness has neither substance nor characteristics,
labeling things as "existent," "nonexistent," "manifest," or "empty" is the perversity of ordinary consciousness.
Therefore, cast off the trap of whatever biases you hold
and understand that unbiased spontaneous presence is like space!

Regardless of what arises to the six avenues of consciousness—appearances seen, sounds heard—
everything is naturally clear, an expanse with no division or exclusion.
Come to this decisive experience within the timelessly free expanse of equalness.

།མཉམ་ཉིད་གཅིག་ལ་ཅིར་སྣང་འབྱུང་བས་དབྱིངས། །ཡོན་ཏན་ཐམས་ཅད་སྐྱིད་པར་བྱེད་པས་གཞི། །ཐམས་ཅད་རང་བྱུང་དབྱེ་བསལ་མེད་པས་ཀློང་། །ཀུན་འབྱུང་སྙིང་པོར་ཤར་བས་བྱང་ཆུབ་སེམས། །མཁའ་འདྲ་གདོད་ནས་དག་པར་ཤེས་པར་བྱ།

།རང་བྱུང་ཡེ་ཤེས་གཞི་ཀློང་ཡངས་པ་ལ། །ཡེ་ནས་དྲི་མེད་འཁོར་བས་མ་གོས་བྱང་། །ཡོན་ཏན་ལྷུན་གྲུབ་རྒྱུ་འབྲས་འདས་པས་ཆུབ། །རང་རིག་སྙིང་པོ་འོད་གསལ་དག་པས་སེམས། །བྱང་ཆུབ་སེམས་སུ་ཀུན་འདུས་རྣམ་པར་དག

།རྩལ་ལས་རོལ་པར་ཤར་བའི་རང་ངོ་ལ། །རྟོགས་པས་གློ་བུར་ཡང་སངས་རྒྱས་པ་དང་། །མ་རྟོགས་མ་རིག་འཁྲུལ་པའི་ཚོགས་ཤར་བས། །ཀུན་གཞི་ལས་མཆེད་ཚོགས་བརྒྱད་ཡུལ་དང་བཅས། །སྣང་སྲིད་སྣོད་བཅུད་རོལ་པར་ཅི་ཤར་ཡང་། །བྱང་ཆུབ་སེམས་ཀྱི་ཀློང་ལས་གཡོས་པ་མེད། །སེམས་ཀློང་མ་གཡོས་མཉམ་པའི་ངང་གནས་ན། །འཁོར་འདས་ཟུང་ཆུབ་དགོངས་ཀློང་ཡངས་པར་གྲོལ།

Awareness is "basic space," because whatever manifests occurs within a single state of equalness.
It is "the ground of being," because it gives rise to all enlightened qualities.
It is "the expanse of being," because everything occurs naturally, without division or exclusion.
It is "awakened mind," because it is experienced as the heart essence that is the source of everything.
You should understand it to be like space, primordially pure.

In the spacious expanse of the ground of being, naturally occurring timeless awareness
is "refined," because it is timelessly immaculate, unsullied by samsara.
It is "consummate," because enlightened qualities are spontaneously present, beyond cause and effect.
It is "mind," because self-knowing awareness is the utterly lucid heart essence.
Everything is subsumed and completely pure within awakened mind.

Within the very essence of what arises as a display due to dynamic energy,
a "reawakening" to buddhahood in the moment comes with realization.
In the absence of realization, thought patterns based on the confusion of nonrecognition arise—
the eight avenues of consciousness that develop from the ground of all ordinary experience, as well as their objects.
Nothing that arises as the display—the entire universe of appearances and possibilities—
strays from the expanse of awakened mind.
If you abide in a state of equalness, without straying from the expanse of mind,
you fully embrace samsara and nirvana, free in the spacious expanse of enlightened intent.

།གཞིས་ལ་འཁོར་འདས་མི་སྲིད་རང་བཞིན་བབས། །བཟང་ངན་བླང་དོར་མི་སྲིད་རང་བཞིན་བབས། །སྤྱངས་ཐོབ་གཟུང་འཛིན་མི་སྲིད་རང་བཞིན་བབས། །དུག་ལྔའི་ཉོན་མོངས་མི་སྲིད་རང་བཞིན་བབས། །རྒྱུ་ཆད་ཕྱོགས་ལྷུང་མི་སྲིད་རང་བཞིན་བབས། །རྩལ་དང་འཆར་བ་མི་སྲིད་རང་བཞིན་བབས། །ཕྱོགས་ཙམ་བཏགས་པ་མི་འགོག་རང་བཞིན་བབས།

།རང་བྱུང་ཡེ་ཤེས་ཆོས་ཟད་མིང་མེད་ལ། །རྩལ་དང་རོལ་པ་ཅི་ཤར་གཞི་མེད་ཉིད། །འཆིང་གྲོལ་མེད་པ་གནས་ལུགས་རང་བཞིན་བབས།། གྲོལ་ཞེས་བརྡར་བཏགས་རང་ཡལ་རྗེས་མེད་ཙམ། །ཀུན་ཡིན་ཀུན་མིན་བཏགས་པར་མི་འགལ་བས། །ཡེ་ནས་གྲོལ་ཞེས་ཚིག་ཏུ་བརྗོད་པ་ཡིན།

།དབྱེ་བསལ་མེད་དོ་ལྷུན་གྲུབ་ཀློང་དུ་གྲོལ། །འདུ་འབྲལ་མེད་དོ་ཐིག་ལེའི་ཀློང་དུ་གྲོལ། །ཅིར་ཡང་འཆར་རོ་ངེས་མེད་ཀློང་དུ་གྲོལ།

།གཟུགས་སུ་སྣང་ངོ་སྣང་བ་རང་སར་གྲོལ། །

The naturally settled state—samsara and nirvana cannot possibly exist within that fundamentally unconditioned state.
The naturally settled state—positive and negative, acceptance and rejection, cannot possibly exist.
The naturally settled state—dualistic perceptions involving renunciation or attainment cannot possibly exist.
The naturally settled state—the five emotional poisons cannot possibly exist.
The naturally settled state—restrictions and extremes cannot possibly exist.
The naturally settled state—dynamic energy and the arising of things cannot possibly exist.
The naturally settled state—there is nothing to prevent it from being labeled, however inadequately.

Within naturally occurring timeless awareness—a state beyond labels, in which phenomena resolve—
whatever arises as its dynamic energy and display is in fact without basis.
The way of abiding, in which there is neither bondage nor freedom, is the naturally settled state.
What is symbolically labeled "freedom" is simply a state in which things vanish naturally, leaving no trace,
and since there is no contradiction in labeling it as anything or nothing,
we describe it with the words "timelessly free."

There is no division or exclusion—there is freedom in the expanse of spontaneous presence.
There is no union or separation—there is freedom in the expanse of the sphere of being.
Anything at all arises—there is freedom in the expanse in which everything is indeterminate.

Forms manifest—sensory appearances are free in their own place.

སྒྲ་རུ་གྲགས་སོ་གྲགས་པ་རང་སར་གྲོལ། །དྲི་རུ་ཚོར་རོ་ཚོར་བ་དབྱིངས་སུ་གྲོལ། །རོ་སྦྱོང་རིག་པ་རང་སའི་ངང་དེར་གྲོལ། །དྲན་རིག་བྱུང་ཚོར་གཞི་རྩ་རྗེན་མེད་གྲོལ།

།གཅིག་ཏུ་གྲོལ་ལོ་ཆོས་ཉིད་ཀློང་དུ་གྲོལ། །གཉིས་སུ་མེད་དོ་ཡུལ་སེམས་མཉམ་པར་གྲོལ། །རང་བྱུང་གྲོལ་ལོ་ཡེ་ཤེས་ཀློང་དུ་གྲོལ། །ལྷུན་གྲུབ་གྲོལ་ལོ་གཞི་དབྱིངས་དག་པར་གྲོལ།

།སྣ་ཚོགས་གྲོལ་ལོ་ཉག་གཅིག་ཀློང་དུ་གྲོལ། །ཕྱོགས་མེད་གྲོལ་ལོ་ལྷུན་གྲུབ་ཀློང་དུ་གྲོལ། །ཐམས་ཅད་གྲོལ་ལོ་སྙིང་པོའི་ཀློང་དུ་གྲོལ།

།འོད་གསལ་གྲོལ་ལོ་ཉི་ཟླའི་ཀློང་དུ་གྲོལ། །ཆོས་ཉིད་གྲོལ་ལོ་ནམ་མཁའི་ཀློང་དུ་གྲོལ། །ཆོས་ཅན་གྲོལ་ལོ་རྒྱ་མཚོའི་ཀློང་དུ་གྲོལ། །མི་འགྱུར་གྲོལ་ལོ་རི་རྒྱལ་ཀློང་དུ་གྲོལ།

།གདོད་ནས་གྲོལ་ལོ་སྐྱེ་མེད་ཀློང་དུ་གྲོལ། །ཕྱམ་གཅིག་གྲོལ་ལོ་ཡེ་སངས་ཀློང་དུ་གྲོལ། །

Sounds are audible—what is audible is free in its own place.
Odors are sensed—sensations are free in basic space.
Flavors are tasted and tactile sensations are felt—they are free
in the context of their own place.
Consciousness and mental events are free, without basis,
foundation, or support.

There is freedom in oneness—freedom in the expanse that is
the true nature of phenomena.
There is no duality—freedom in the equalness of sense objects
and mind.
There is naturally occurring freedom—freedom in the expanse
of timeless awareness.
There is spontaneously present freedom—freedom in the purity
of the ground of being as basic space.

There is freedom in the variety of things—freedom within the
unique expanse.
There is freedom not subject to extremes—freedom within the
spontaneously present expanse.
There is universal freedom—freedom within the expanse
of the heart essence.

There is freedom as utter lucidity—freedom within the expanse
of the sun and moon.
There is freedom as the true nature of phenomena—freedom
within the expanse of space.
There is freedom of objects in the phenomenal world—freedom
within the expanse of the ocean.
There is unchanging freedom—freedom within the expanse of
the most majestic mountain.

There is primordial freedom—freedom in the unborn expanse.
There is freedom in the single state of evenness—freedom in the
expanse of timeless awakening.

ཡོངས་གྲོལ་གྲོལ་ལོ་ཡེ་རྒྱས་ཀློང་དུ་གྲོལ།

།ཆོས་དབྱིངས་རིན་པོ་ཆེའི་མཛོད་ལས། །ཆོས་ཐམས་ཅད་བྱང་ཆུབ་སེམས་སུ་ཡེ་ནས་གྲོལ་བའི་རང་བཞིན་བསྟན་པའི་ལེའུ་སྟེ་བཅུ་གཉིས་པའོ།།

།།ཆོས་རྣམས་ལྷུན་གྲུབ་བྱང་ཆུབ་སྙིང་པོ་ལ། །འབད་རྩོལ་མེད་པའི་གནད་ཀྱིས་གོམས་བྱས་ན། །ཡེ་སངས་རྒྱས་ལ་ཡང་སངས་རྒྱས་འབྱུང་སྟེ། །འདི་ནི་བླ་མེད་རྡོ་རྗེ་སྙིང་པོའི་རྩེ། །རིམ་དགུའི་སྙིང་པོ་བྱང་ཆུབ་ཀློང་ཆེན་ཡིན།

།མཁའ་དཀྱིལ་ཉི་ཟླའི་དཀྱིལ་འཁོར་འོད་གསལ་ཡང་། །མ་རྟོགས་སྤྲིན་ཆེན་སྙིང་པོས་ཡོངས་བསྒྲིབས་པས། །མི་སྣང་བྱང་ཆུབ་རང་ལ་ཡོད་པའི་ཚུལ།

།སྤྲིན་ཆེན་དབྱིངས་སུ་བཞག་པས་རང་དེངས་ལྟར། །འབད་རྩོལ་མེད་པས་རྒྱུ་འབྲས་སྤྲིན་བྲལ་ནས། །མཁའ་དཀྱིལ་བྱང་ཆུབ་སྙིང་པོ་རང་ལས་འཆར། །དབང་པོའི་རིམ་པས་ཐེག་པ་ཐ་དད་ལ།

།ངོ་བོ་ཉི་བཞིན་ཆོས་དབྱིངས་ཀློང་ན་གསལ།

།

There is total freedom—freedom in the timelessly unfolding
expanse.

This is the twelfth section of *The Precious Treasury of the Basic Space of Phenomena,* demonstrating that all phenomena are by nature timelessly free in awakened mind.

❖

IF, THROUGH THE KEY POINT of effortlessness, there is familiarity
with the very essence of enlightenment—the spontaneous presence of phenomena—
although buddhahood is timeless, there is awakening to buddhahood anew.
This is the unsurpassable pinnacle of the vajra heart essence—
the vast expanse of enlightenment, the very essence of the nine progressive approaches.

Although the orbs of the sun and moon are radiantly luminous in the vault of the sky,
they can be completely obscured by thick clouds, which prevents them from being seen.
This parallels the way in which enlightenment, though present within you, is not apparent.

Thick clouds vanish naturally when left alone in the sky.
Similarly, the clouds of causality vanish without effort or striving,
and the very essence of enlightenment shines in and of itself in the vault of the sky.
Given the varying degrees of acumen, there are different spiritual approaches.

The essence is like the sun, shining clearly in the expanse of the basic space of phenomena.

རྩལ་ལས་ཟེར་བཞིན་ཀུན་ཤར་རིས་མེད་པས། །ས་དང་ཆུ་མཚོར་དྲོད་ཀྱིས་ཁྱབ་པ་ན། །རླངས་ལས་སྤྲིན་གྱི་རོལ་པར་ཤར་བ་ཡིས། །ངོ་བོ་ཉིད་དང་རྩལ་ཡང་བསྒྲིབས་པ་བཞིན། །ངོ་བོ་ཉིད་ལས་རང་རྩལ་མ་དག་པའི། །རོལ་པས་སྙིང་པོའི་དེ་ཉིད་རང་ངོར་བསྒྲིབས། །སྣང་སྲིད་སྣོད་བཅུད་འཁྲུལ་སྣང་བསམ་མི་ཁྱབ།

།ཉི་ཟེར་རྩལ་ལས་རླུང་བསྐྱོད་སྤྲིན་དེངས་ལྟར། །རང་ངོ་རྟོགས་ལས་རོལ་པ་རྒྱན་དུ་ཤར། །འཁྲུལ་པ་ཡི་གྲོལ་རང་སར་དག་གྲོལ་བས། །འཁྲུལ་སྣང་འཁྲུལ་འཛིན་མ་སྤྱངས་དབྱིངས་སུ་དག །ཀར་སོང་ཆ་མེད་དངས་པའི་ནམ་མཁའ་ལ། །སྐུ་དང་ཡེ་ཤེས་ལྷུན་གྲུབ་ཉི་མ་ཤར། །གཞན་ནས་མ་འོངས་རང་སྣང་དག་པ་ཙམ།

།གཉིས་སྐྱེས་སྒོ་ངའི་ནང་ནས་འདབ་རྒྱས་པ། །སྒོང་རྒྱས་འཐུམས་ལྟར་ད་ལྟར་མི་སྣང་ཡང་། །སྒོང་རྒྱ་རལ་བས་མཁའ་དཀྱིལ་ལྡིང་བ་ལྟར། །གཟུང་འཛིན་འཁྲུལ་རྟོག་ཟག་པ་སྤུར་ཟད་ཀྱང་། །ཟག་འབྲས་ལྷག་བཅས་སྒོང་རྒྱ་རལ་མ་ཐག །ལྷུན་གྲུབ་རིག་པ་རང་གསལ་རང་ལ་འཆར། །སྐུ་དང་ཡེ་ཤེས་སྣང་བས་མཁའ་དབྱིངས་ཁྱབ། །

Everything arises without bias due to its dynamic energy,
which is like the sun's rays.
They suffuse the earth and bodies of water with warmth,
so that a display of clouds arises, formed from water vapor.
This obscures the essence itself and even its dynamic energy.
Similarly, due to the impure display of natural dynamic energy
deriving from the essence itself,
one's perception of suchness, the heart essence, is obscured.
The universe of appearances and possibilities consists of
an inconceivable range of perceptions based on confusion.

The dynamic energy of the sun's rays stirs the wind that
disperses clouds.
Similarly, with the realization of the very essence of being,
its display is experienced as its adornment.
Confusion, which has always been free, is now free in its
own place.
Confused perception and reification are purified in basic space
without having to be renounced.
You have no idea where they have gone.
The spontaneously present sun shines as the kayas and timeless
awareness in the limpid sky.
It does not come from somewhere else, but is simply awareness's
own pure manifestation.

The wings of a garuda unfold within the egg.
As long as it is enveloped by the shell, this is not evident,
but when the shell breaks, the garuda soars into the vault
of the sky.
Similarly, although the contamination of confused dualistic
thinking has already resolved,
when the "shell"—the result of this contamination—breaks,
spontaneously present awareness immediately arises in and of
itself, naturally lucid.
The vast perspective of the kayas and timeless awareness fills
the "sky" of basic space.

རང་ངོ་ཤེས་པས་ཀུན་བཟང་ཀློང་དུ་གྲོལ།

།ཕྱོགས་བཅུར་ཐུགས་རྗེའི་རོལ་པ་ཚད་མེད་ལས། །སྤྲུལ་པ་འཕྲོ་བས་འགྲོ་བའི་དོན་ཀུན་བྱེད། །འཁོར་བ་ཇི་སྲིད་མཛད་པ་ཉེ་བར་སྟོན། །འདི་ནི་རང་བཞིན་བབས་ཀྱི་ངོ་བོ་ལས། །རྩལ་གྱི་ཐུགས་རྗེ་ཕྱོགས་མེད་ཤར་བ་ལས། །རོལ་པས་གཞན་དོན་ཕུན་སུམ་ཚོགས་པ་ཡིན།

།མ་དག་ཆ་བཅས་རོལ་པ་ཉེར་ཞི་ཡང་། །མ་དག་འགྲོ་ལ་སྤྲུལ་པ་སྣང་བ་ནི། །སྟོན་པའི་ཇི་བཞིན་ཤུགས་ཀྱི་ཐུགས་རྗེ་དང་། །འགྲོ་སེམས་གཙང་མའི་ལས་སྨོན་དག་པས་འཆར།

།དེ་ཚེ་ཞིང་ཀུན་སྤྲུལ་པ་ཚད་མེད་ཅིང་། །མཐའ་ཡས་འགྲོ་བ་བྱང་ཆུབ་འདྲེན་མཛད་ཀྱང་། །སྟོན་པའི་ཆོས་སྐུ་དབྱིངས་ལས་མི་གཡོ་སྟེ། །རང་བྱུང་ཡེ་ཤེས་རྒྱ་ཆད་ཕྱོགས་ལྷུང་མེད། །དབྱིངས་ལས་རང་ཤར་སྟུག་པོ་བཀོད་པར་ནི། །རིག་འཛིན་མཁའ་འགྲོ་ས་བཅུའི་སེམས་དཔའ་ལ། །ལོངས་སྤྱོད་རྫོགས་པའི་བཀོད་པ་བསམ་ཡས་སྣང་། །དེ་ཡང་དབྱིངས་ལས་སྟོན་པའི་ཐུགས་རྗེ་དང་། །གདུལ་བྱའི་མོས་དགེས་ལྷུན་གྲུབ་རང་ངོར་སྣང་།

With recognition of the very essence of being comes freedom
within the expanse of Samantabhadra.

Since the display of responsiveness is immeasurable throughout
the ten directions,
emanations issue forth to ensure total benefit for beings.
Enlightened actions are revealed for as long as samsara lasts.
This is impartial responsiveness, dynamic energy arising
from the naturally settled essence of being
so that through its display there is abundant benefit for others.

Although the impure display, along with all it entails,
thoroughly subsides,
emanations manifest for beings in impure states.
They arise out of the responsiveness of teachers—a power
that is simply so—
and the pure karma and aspirations of beings with positive
minds.

At that point, although there are innumerable emanations
in all realms,
leading countless beings to enlightenment,
they do not stray from basic space—the dharmakaya of
the teachers.
Naturally occurring timeless awareness is not subject to
restrictions or extremes.
Arising naturally within basic space, in the realm of
Ghanavyuha,
an inconceivable array of the sambhogakaya manifests
to masters of awareness, dakas and dakinis, and bodhisattvas
on the tenth level of realization.
Moreover, it manifests within basic space as the very essence
of spontaneous presence,
due to the responsiveness of teachers and the inspiration and
virtue of those to be guided.

།ཆོས་སྐུའི་ངོ་བོ་རང་བྱུང་ཡེ་ཤེས་ཏེ། །རོལ་པར་ཐམས་ཅད་མཁྱེན་པའི་ཡེ་ཤེས་མཆོག །གདོད་མའི་དབྱིངས་ན་ཐིག་ལེ་གཅིག་ཏུ་བཞུགས།

།ལོངས་སྐུའི་ངོ་བོ་རང་བཞིན་ལྷུན་གྲུབ་སྟེ། །རོལ་པར་རིགས་ལྔ་ཡེ་ཤེས་རྣམ་པ་ལྔ། །ནམ་མཁའི་དབྱིངས་ཀུན་གང་བར་སྣང་བ་ཡིན།

།སྤྲུལ་སྐུའི་ངོ་བོ་ཐུགས་རྗེའི་འཆར་གཞི་སྟེ། །རོལ་པར་གང་ལ་གང་འདུལ་དེར་སྣང་ཞིང་། །འཕྲིན་ལས་ཆེན་པོས་མངའ་དབང་འགྱུར་པ་ཡིན།

།འདི་དག་རྒྱུ་འབྲས་རྩོལ་བས་མ་བསྒྲུབས་ཏེ། །ཡེ་ནས་ལྷུན་གྲུབ་ཅོག་གཞག་ངང་ལ་སྣང་། །མཆོག་གསང་རབ་ལ་ཚེ་འདིར་སྣང་བ་སྟེ། །དེ་ལས་གཞན་དུ་བར་དོར་མི་བསླུ་བས། །རྡོ་རྗེ་སྙིང་པོ་རྩེ་མོའི་ཐེག་པ་ནི། །རྒྱུ་འབྲས་ཐེག་པ་ཀུན་ལས་ཁྱད་པར་འཕགས།

།ཆོས་དབྱིངས་རིན་པོ་ཆེའི་མཛོད་ལས། །ཆོས་ཐམས་ཅད་བྱང་ཆུབ་ཀྱི་སེམས་སུ་ཡེ་སངས་རྒྱས་པ་ལ་རྩོལ་བ་དང་སྒྲུབ་པ་མེད་པར་ཡང་སངས་རྒྱས་པར་བསྟན་པའི་ལེའུ་སྟེ་བཅུ་གསུམ་པའོ།།

།།དེ་ལྟར་ཆོས་ཉིད་རྡོ་རྗེ་སྙིང་པོའི་གླུ། །མཁའ་མཉམ་གདོད་ནས་དག་པའི་རང་བཞིན་འདི།

།

The essence of dharmakaya is naturally occurring timeless awareness.
Its display is the reservoir of omniscient timeless awareness,
abiding as the single sphere of being within primordial basic space.

The essence of sambhogakaya is the spontaneously present nature of being.
Its display is the five buddha families and the five aspects of timeless awareness,
manifesting to fill all realms of space.

The essence of nirmanakaya is the ground for the arising of responsiveness.
Its display manifests in whatever way is necessary to guide under any circumstances,
while its supreme enlightened activity brings mastery.

The kayas are not achieved by effort involving cause and effect.
They are timelessly and spontaneously present, manifesting within a state of resting imperturbably.
The most sublime secret manifests in this lifetime.
You are not lured away from it in the interval after death,
and so the pinnacle approach of the vajra heart essence
is exalted above all other approaches, based as they are on causes or results.

This is the thirteenth section of *The Precious Treasury of the Basic Space of Phenomena,* demonstrating that, since all phenomena already constitute the timelessly awakened state of buddhahood, awakening to buddhahood anew happens without effort or achievement.

❖

SUCH IS THE SONG of the vajra heart essence—the true nature of phenomena.
This primordially pure nature, equal to space,

མི་འགྱུར་གཞི་རྩ་བྲལ་བའི་གནས་ཉིད་དུ། །རང་ཤར་འཕོ་འགྱུར་མེད་པའི་རོལ་པར་ཤར།

།ཡི་མཉམ་ཕྱམ་གདལ་ཀློང་ཆེན་ཡངས་པའི་དོན། །གར་ཡང་མ་ཕྱིན་གདོད་མའི་རང་བཞིན་དང་། །མི་གཡོ་ལྷུན་གྱིས་གྲུབ་པའི་ཆོས་ཉིད་ལ། །རྒྱ་ཆད་མེད་ཅིང་ཕྱོགས་ལྷུང་བྲལ་བར་གྱུར།

།དོན་རྣམས་ཛཱ་བཞིན་མཁའ་མཉམ་ཡངས་པའི་དཀྱིལ། །གང་དུ་རང་བྱུང་ཀློང་ཆེན་རྒྱལ་པོ་ནི། །རྟག་ཏུ་མི་གཡོ་སྣ་ཚོགས་རང་སར་གྲོལ། །འདི་ཞེས་མི་མཚོན་དབྱིངས་རུམ་ཡངས་པར་ཕྱིན།

།རྫོགས་པའི་དུས་ངེས་མཁའ་འདྲའི་རྣལ་འབྱོར་པས། །རང་ཉམས་ཕྱོགས་གཅིག་ལུང་དོན་མཐུན་པ་ནི། །རྩ་བའི་སེམས་ལུང་ཉི་ཤུ་རྩ་གཅིག་དང་། །ཀློང་གསུམ་མན་ངག་སྡེ་བཞི་མཐུན་པར་བཀོད།

།དགེ་བ་དེ་ཡིས་མ་ལུས་འགྲོ་བ་ཀུན། །མ་འབད་བཞིན་དུ་གདོད་མའི་སར་ཕྱིན་ནས། །ཀུན་བཟང་ས་ལ་འཕོ་འགྱུར་མེད་པ་ཡི། །དོན་གཉིས་ལྷུན་གྲུབ་ཆོས་ཀྱི་རྒྱལ་པོར་ཤོག

arises naturally in the unchanging environment free of
underlying basis or foundation,
becoming apparent as a display that is without transition
or change.

This is the meaning of the spacious, supreme expanse of being,
an infinite state of timeless equalness.
Without having gone anywhere, you reach your primordial
nature.
This true nature, unwavering and spontaneously present,
is not subject to restrictions and is free of bias.

The meanings concern the spacious realm equal to space,
just as it is.
There, the monarch of the naturally occurring vast expanse
never wavers, free in the natural state of things in all their
variety.
I have reached the ultimate womb of basic space, which cannot
be characterized as some "thing."

When my realization was certain, I, a yogin who is like the sky,
wrote this summation of my own experience, together with
appropriate scriptural citations,
setting it down in accord with the twenty-one transmissions of
the Category of Mind,
the three sections of the Category of Expanse, and the four
sections of the Category of Direct Transmission.

By this virtue, may all beings without exception
effortlessly reach the primordial ground.
May they become spiritual rulers who spontaneously accomplish
the two kinds of benefit,
dwelling on the level of Samantabhadra without transition
or change!

།ཕྱོགས་རྣམས་ཀུན་ཏུ་བདེ་དཔལ་འབྱོར་པ་ནི། །དག་པའི་ཞིང་བཞིན་འདོད་དགུ་ལྷུན་གྲུབ་ཅིང་། །ཆོས་ཛ་སྒྲོགས་པས་ཐར་པའི་རྒྱལ་མཚན་འཛུགས། །དམ་ཆོས་མི་ནུབ་བསྟན་པ་དར་རྒྱས་ཤོག

།ཆོས་དབྱིངས་རིན་པོ་ཆེའི་མཛོད་ཅེས་བྱ་བ། །ཐེག་པ་མཆོག་གི་རྣལ་འབྱོར་པ་ཀློང་ཆེན་རབ་འབྱམས་ཀྱིས་གངས་རི་ཐོད་དཀར་གྱི་མགུལ་དུ་ལེགས་པར་བཀོད་པ་རྫོགས་སོ།།

།།དགེའོ། །དགེའོ། །དགེའོ།།

In all directions, may there be well-being, splendor, and wealth,
so that everything that is wished for is spontaneously
accomplished, as though in a pure realm.
May the drum of spiritual teachings resound and the victory
banner of liberation be raised.
May the sacred teachings never wane, but spread and flourish!

This text, entitled *The Precious Treasury of the Basic Space of Phenomena,* composed on the slopes of Gangri Tökar by a yogin of the most sublime spiritual approach, Longchen Rabjam, is now completely finished.

❖

Good fortune! Good fortune! Good fortune!